THE CATHOLIC UNIVERSITY OF AMERICA
CANON LAW STUDIES
No. 295

THE OBLIGATION OF HOLDING SACRED MISSIONS IN PARISHES

A HISTORICAL SYNOPSIS AND A COMMENTARY

By

REV. HOWARD DAVID LAVELLE, A.B., J.C.L.
Priest of the Diocese of Seattle

A DISSERTATION

Submitted to the Faculty of the School of Canon Law of the Catholic University of America in Partial Fulfillment of the Requirements for the Degree of Doctor of Canon Law

THE CATHOLIC UNIVERSITY OF AMERICA PRESS
WASHINGTON, D. C.
1949

Nihil Obstat:

EDUARDUS G. ROELKER, S.T.D., J.C.D.,
Censor Deputatus.

Washingtonii, D. C., die 24 Maii, 1949.

Imprimatur:

✠ THOMAS A. CONNOLLY, D.D., J.C.D.,
Episcopus Seattlensis Coadjutor.

Seattli, die 24 Maii, 1949.

Printed by
THE PAULIST PRESS
401 WEST 59TH STREET
NEW YORK 19, N. Y.

51

TO MY MOTHER

AND

IN MEMORY OF

MY FATHER

TABLE OF CONTENTS

CHAPTER VII

CHAPTER VIII

CHAPTER IX

CHAPTER X

FOREWORD

One of the most beneficial events in the life of a modern parish is the periodic parochial or sacred mission. The attendance at such a mission is generally very good. There is something about this type of spiritual exercises which attracts the interest and devotion of men, women, and children alike. If the mission is well-given and well-attended, the beneficial effects, in elevating the spiritual life of the parish, will soon be manifested by a more frequent reception of the sacraments, and especially by a penitential return of sinners to the conscientious practice of their Faith.

The first part of this dissertation deals with the development of sacred missions and with the gradual rise of the obligation of holding them in parishes. Sacred missions, as such, are of comparatively recent origin, dating only from the late sixteenth century. The universal obligation of holding missions in parishes began only with the Code of Canon Law.

The history of the subject falls naturally into five periods: preaching during the first twelve centuries after Christ, the rise of popular preaching from the thirteenth to the seventeenth century, the organization and progress of sacred missions from the seventeenth to the nineteenth century, the rise of the obligation in the nineteenth century, and the determination of the obligation in the twentieth century. The method used for illustrating the history of sacred missions in each of these periods is to examine first the development and characteristics of the preaching or mission activity, and then the pertinent legislation of each period.

The second part of this dissertation consists in a commentary on the canonical obligation of holding sacred missions in parishes. Canon 1349 states the obligation, and therefore it is treated at length. Particular legislation plays a very important rôle in determining the obligation of holding sacred missions. Consequently, considerable attention is given to the laws on sacred missions enacted by various councils and synods. The means of enforcing the obligation are also examined. Since there are many kinds of spiritual exercises which closely resemble sacred missions, a brief treatment is devoted to each of the principal types.

The importance and value of sacred missions for the faithful can hardly be over-estimated. These missions are as necessary for the laity as retreats are for the clergy. It is hoped that this study, in emphasizing the obligation, will also serve to point out the great value of holding sacred missions in the parishes.

The writer wishes here to express his appreciation to all who have helped him in making this work possible: to Their Excellencies, the Most Reverend Gerald Shaughnessy, S.M., S.T.D., and the Most Reverend Thomas A. Connolly, D.D., J.C.D., for the opportunity of pursuing the study of Canon Law at the Catholic University of America; to the Faculty of the School of Canon Law for their guidance and assistance; to the Fathers and Scholastics of Marist College and Seminary, Washington, D. C., for their kindness and help; and to all others unnamed who have given of their time and talents toward the completion of this study.

PRELIMINARY NOTIONS

The Derivation and Various Meanings of the Word Mission

The word mission (Lat. *missio*, from *mittere*, to send) is used in various ways. In general, a mission means that with which a messenger or agent is charged.[1] Thus a special envoy or delegate, sent by one country to another for a particular purpose, is often said to have undertaken a mission. Sometimes the word mission is used as a synonym for vocation. Evangelical Protestant sects frequently call their revival meetings missions, and their meeting houses in slum districts are also called missions.[2]

The Catholic Church also uses the term mission in different senses. The early churches in California, founded by Father Junípero Serra (1713-1784) and his fellow Franciscans, were called missions, and from these churches we have such expressions as *mission* furniture and the *mission* style of architecture.[3] The name mission is commonly given also to any church which does not have a resident pastor but is attended from the parish in which it is located.[4]

The term *canonical mission* refers to the permission to preach, which must be obtained from the ordinary of the place or some other lawful superior.[5] The simplest territorial organization in the

[1] *New International Dictionary* (Second Unabridged Edition, Springfield, Mass.: G. & C. Merriam Co., 1941), p. 1571.

[2] Schmidlin, *Catholic Mission Theory* (translated by Matthias Braun, Techny, Ill.: Mission Press, 1931), pp. 34-37.

[3] "California Missions,"—*The New Catholic Dictionary* (New York: The Universal Knowledge Foundation, 1929), p. 637.

[4] Can. 1182.—§ 2. Etiam oblationes factas in commodum paroeciae aut missionis, aut ecclesiae sitae intra paroeciae vel missionis fines, administrat parochus vel missionarius. . . .

[5] Can. 1328.—Nemini ministerium praedicationis licet exercere, nisi a legitimo Superiore missionem receperit, facultate peculiariter data, vel officio collato, cui ex sacris canonibus praedicandi munus inhaereat.

Church is also called a mission. In countries which are directly under the control of the Sacred Congregation for the Propagation of the Faith, the ecclesiastical divisions are called missions until they become sufficiently developed. They are then erected by the Holy See into prefectures apostolic, vicariates apostolic, and finally dioceses.[6] Those who are ordained to serve in places which are under the supervision of the Sacred Congregation for the Propagation of the Faith are ordained with the title of mission.[7]

Often the word mission is used in reference to the whole priestly work, even though the country is no longer under the jurisdiction of the Congregation for the Propagation of the Faith. This usage is common among priests of English or Irish ancestry, who refer to a priest in parish work as being "on the mission." [8]

The term missions, used broadly, includes all the activities which the Church uses in its endeavors to spread the Catholic Faith in foreign lands as well as at home.[9] Missions, then, may be said to be sacred enterprises which are instituted directly either for the renewing of Christian fervor and the converting of sinners among the faithful, or for the spreading of the Catholic Faith among heretics or infidels. The distinction should be made, therefore, between *external* missions, which are undertaken in non-Catholic or infidel lands, and *internal* missions, which are given in Catholic regions.[10]

THE NOTION AND PURPOSE OF SACRED MISSIONS

This dissertation is concerned specifically with the internal or sacred missions [11] as they are mentioned in the Code of Canon

[6] Can. 215, § 1.

[7] Can. 981.—§ 1. Si ne unus quidem ex titulis de quibus in can. 979, § 1, praesto sit, suppleri potest titulo missionis, ita tamen ut ordinatus, iureiurando interposito, se devoveat perpetuo dioecesis aut missionis servitio, sub Ordinarii loci pro tempore auctoritate.

[8] E.g., the title of the book by Frederick Oakeley (1802-1880), *The Priest on the Mission, A Course of Lectures on Missionary and Parochial Duties* (London: Longmans, Green & Co., 1871).

[9] Schmidlin, *Catholic Mission Theory,* pp. 34-39.

[10] Vermeersch-Creusen, *Epitome Iuris Canonici* (6. ed., 3 vols., Mechliniae et Romae: H. Dessain, 1937-1946), II, 473-474.

[11] These missions are known also under other names: popular missions,

Law.[12] Such a sacred mission consists in an extraordinary and well-ordered series of sermons, instructions, and spiritual exercises coupled with the frequentation of the sacraments,[13] continued in a parish or a community for a week or more with the approval of the ordinary of the place and the pastor or other proper superior.[14]

The purpose of sacred missions is to instruct Catholics more fully in the truths of their religion, to convert sinners, to rouse the torpid and indifferent, and to lift the good to a still higher plane of spiritual effort.[15]

The occasion of a sacred mission also provides an opportunity for the instruction of non-Catholics. Catholics are often urged to bring their non-Catholic friends and relatives to the mission. Sometimes missions are held specifically for non-Catholics.[16]

This dissertation will deal primarily with Catholic missions, and the term sacred missions will refer exclusively to the missions for the faithful. Parochial retreats and days of recollection, conferences, and non-Catholic missions will be treated separately from sacred missions in this dissertation. The Code does not mention retreats or such spiritual exercises for the laity, nor does it mention missions for non-Catholics, other than to state that some provision should be made for non-Catholics.[17]

sacred expeditions, popular spiritual exercises, spiritual exercise of the missions, parochial retreats, parochial missions, and parish missions.—Hinschius, *System des katholischen Kirchenrechts* (4 vols., Berlin: Guttentag, 1869-1888), IV, 486; McVann, *The Canon Law on Sermon Preaching* (New York: Paulist Press, 1940), p. 149 (hereafter cited McVann).

12 Can. 1349.—§ 1. Ordinarii advigilent ut, saltem decimo quoque anno, sacram, quam vocant, missionem, ad gregem sibi commissum habendam parochi curent.

13 Beste, *Introductio in Codicem* (3. ed., Collegeville, Minn.: St. John's Abbey Press, 1946), p. 674.

14 Coronata, *Institutiones Iuris Canonici* (2. ed., 5 vols., Romae: Marietti, 1939-1947), II, 273 (hereafter cited Coronata).

15 Schroeder, "Mission, parochial"—*The Catholic Encyclopedia* (15 vols., Index, and two Supplements, New York, 1907-1921), X, 391-394 (hereafter cited *CE*).

16 Ayrinhac, *Administrative Legislation in the New Code of Canon Law* (New York: Longmans, Green & Co., 1930), pp. 231-232.

17 Can. 1350.—§ 1. Ordinarii locorum et parochi acatholicos, in suis dioecesibus et paroeciis degentes, commendatos sibi in Domino habeant.

Part I

Historical Synopsis

CHAPTER I

THE HISTORICAL DEVELOPMENT BEFORE THE THIRTEENTH CENTURY

In tracing the early history of sacred missions, one notes that the work of the home and of the foreign missions was practically identified. Sacred missions, intended specifically for the faithful, did not exist in any organized form until the seventeenth century. The gradual development, however, of the idea of popular missions can be observed through the preceding centuries from the time of Christ until the thirteenth century, when popular missionary endeavor became intensified.

Article 1. Christ and His Apostles

When Our Lord began His public life at the age of thirty, He became the first missionary in the Church which He founded. From the beginning of His public ministry, "Jesus began to preach and to say, 'Repent for the kingdom of heaven is at hand.' "[1] At the close of His life's work He entrusted its continuation to His Apostles, "going therefore, teach ye all nations . . . teaching them to observe all things whatsoever I have commanded you."[2]

The early Church tried to carry out the instructions of Our Lord to preach the Gospel to all nations. The Apostles, in particular St. Peter and St. Paul, carried the Gospel over the then known

[1] St. Matthew, IV: 17—*The New Testament of Our Lord and Saviour Jesus Christ,* a Revision of the Challoner-Rheims Version by the Confraternity of Christian Doctrine (Paterson, N. J.: St. Anthony Guild Press, 1941); (hereafter used for all N.T. citations).

[2] Matt., XXVIII: 19, 20.

world. Religious instruction was carried on in the churches which they founded, and visits by the Apostles to these churches were always the occasion of renewed religious fervor, which may be regarded as the first antecedents of the present day popular missions. The Apostles were assisted in this work by the charismatic workers who traveled about giving instruction in the Faith. Large crowds of the faithful gathered to hear them whenever they preached, in view of the marvelous powers of speech which were given them through the power of the Holy Ghost.[3]

Article 2. The Fathers of the Church

The beginning of popular missionary work can be noticed even among the Fathers of the Church such as Saints Gregory Nazianzus (ca. 329-390), Gregory of Nyssa (ca. 331-395), Basil (329-379), John Chrysostom (ca. 344-407), Ambrose (ca. 340-397), Augustine (354-430) and Leo (ca. 390-461). Preaching in the early Church was primarily the task of bishops.[4] They preached throughout their dioceses, and often their eloquence was so great that their sermons were the occasion of renewed religious enthusiasm and activity. The early Christian communities were surrounded by paganism, and they needed to be periodically checked to prevent them from falling into heresy or idolatry. They were without books, and there were very few Christian schools. In consequence the faithful depended almost entirely upon the sermons of their bishops and priests for religious instruction and inspiration.[5]

Article 3. Conversion of Europe

The conversion of Ireland, Scotland, and England took place in the fifth and sixth centuries largely through the efforts of St. Pat-

[3] Batiffol, *Primitive Catholicism* (translated by H. L. Brianceau, New York: Longmans, Green & Co., 1911), pp. 29-30; Mourret-Thompson, *A History of the Catholic Church* (6 vols. published, St. Louis: Herder, 1930-1945), I, 43, 58, 82 (hereafter cited Mourret).

[4] Thomassinus, *Vetus et Nova Disciplina circa Beneficia et Beneficarios* (Lugduni, 1706), Pars III, Lib. 1, cap. 40, n. 7, § Ne; McVann, p. 8.

[5] Schroeder, "Missions, parochial"—*CE,* X, 392; Dargan, *History of Preaching* (New York: A. C. Armstrong & Son, 1905), p. 35.

rick (ca. 389-ca. 461) and his companions, and from these islands spread a corps of missionaries who did much to spread the Faith in Europe among pagans, and who through their work with those who had already been converted became in a sense an early type of the popular missionaries. Some of the outstanding missionaries were Saints Fridolin (+ ca. 538), Columban (ca. 543-615), Gall (ca. 550-ca. 645), Kilian (+ ca. 689), and their companions. Upon the conversion of the communities the first care of the missionaries was to create as soon as possible permanent centers around which the ecclesiastical life would revolve; hence they built churches, installed priests, organized Christian communities. They then revisited these centers to encourage the neophytes and to help them progress in their newly-found Faith.[6]

St. Boniface (ca. 680-754) became known as the Apostle of Germany because of his untiring efforts to evangelize the Germanic tribes. Some of the converts made by St. Boniface and his fellow missionaries soon fell away from the Faith as a result of the pagan environment in which they lived. In 723 St. Boniface was appointed, by Pope Gregory II (715-731), as Archbishop of the German provinces in which he had been laboring. In the letter which announced the appointment of St. Boniface to the bishops, the clergy, and the laity of the Germanic territories, the Pope emphasized the fact that besides the work of converting infidels, there was also the special work of properly instructing the Christians and of bringing back those who had fallen away. The Pope indicated that Christians were to be instructed in their Faith by means of the systematic preaching of the Gospel and of the doctrines of the Catholic religion.[7]

Preaching to all classes of people was urged by many of the

[6] Mourret, II, 145-239; Schmidlin, *Catholic Mission History* (translated by Matthias Braun, Techny, Ill.: Mission Press, 1933), pp. 157-222; Wetenkampf, *Catholic Missions in the Early Middle Ages* (New York: The Society for the Propagatiion of the Faith, 1944), pp. 155-160.

[7] Epistola III Gregorii Papae III—Migne, *Patrologiae Cursus Completus, Series Latina* (221 vols., Parisiis, 1844-1864), LXXXIX, 501 (hereafter cited *MPL*). For a more complete account of the missionary activity of St. Boniface, confer Robinson, *Life of Saint Boniface by Willibald* (Cambridge, Mass.: Harvard U. Press, 1917).

councils, and it received special impetus through the *Regula Pastoralis* of Pope St. Gregory the Great (590-604),[8] which served as a handbook for preachers and as a guide for the legislation on preaching in these councils.[9] This great work had a profound effect upon the development of preaching and was frequently quoted by succeeding authors.

Article 4. Preaching for the Crusades

In the eleventh century the Moslems, especially the Turks, had overrun the East, including the Holy Land, and were rapidly becoming a serious threat to the Christian countries of Europe. In order to halt the Moslem advance and in an endeavor to recover the Holy Land from the infidels, Pope Urban II (1088-1099), at the Council of Clermont in 1095, called all of the Christian people to arms.[10]

The call was enthusiastically answered, and the movement became known as the First Crusade. Some of the more prominent figures who preached in the First Crusade and in the succeeding Crusades were Peter the Hermit (1050-1115), St. Bernard (1091-1153), Peter Comestor (+1179), and Peter Cantor (+1197), and Foulques de Neuilly (+1199). Their appeals to the Christian zeal of Europe were splendid instances of popular missions adapted to the conditions of the age. It should be noted that they preached in behalf of the Crusades at the command and under the direction of the various Popes during whose pontificates the Crusades took place.[11]

[8] *MPL*, LXXVIII, 13-125; text and commentary also in Hedley, *Lex Levitarum* (London: Westminster Art and Book Co., 1905), pp. 163-349.

[9] Rheims (ca. 630), Cap. I, can. 19—Labbeus-Cossartius, *Sacrosancta Concilia ad Regiam Editionem Exacta* (17 vols., Lutetiae Parisiorum, 1671-1672), V, 1693 (hereafter cited Labbeus-Cossartius); Toledo IX (655), Cap. I, can. 4,—*op. cit.*, VI, 452; Aachen II (836), Cap. II, can. 3-6,—*op. cit.*, VIII, 1708.

[10] Labbeus-Cossartius, VIII, 1708.

[11] Mourret, IV, 280-285, 361-366, 536-545.

CHAPTER II

FROM THE THIRTEENTH TO THE SEVENTEENTH CENTURY

THE thirteenth century marked the beginning of a new style of preaching in the Catholic Church. That contrast one will note in comparing the development in the thirteenth century with that in the preceding twelve centuries.

ARTICLE 1. ATTITUDE OF THE HOLY SEE ON PREACHING IN GENERAL

A. The Bishops and the Secular Clergy

Throughout the first twelve centuries, preaching was considered primarily the privilege and duty of the bishops. If they were impeded from performing this apostolic work, then the obligation rested upon them to see that qualified preachers were appointed to explain the word of God to the people. This obligation was stressed by several councils of the Church.[1] The bishops were expected to confine their preaching to their own dioceses and were not to enter other dioceses unless they were invited to do so.

B. The Monastic Orders

The early hermits and monks in the Catholic Church, following first the Rule of St. Basil (329-379) and later the Rule of St. Benedict (480-547), confined themselves to their monasteries in order to develop their own spiritual lives, and to undertake research

[1] Chalcedon (451), can. 4, *in epistola Alexandri II ad plebem Florentinam*, c. 11, C. XVI, q. 1—*Corpus Iuris Canonici* (Editio Lipsiensis II, Richter-Friedberg, 2 vols., Lipsiae, 1879-1881, editio anastatice repetita, Lipsiae: Tauchnitz, 1922), n. 73, coll. 763-764; Tarragona (516), Cap. XI—Hardouin, *Acta Conciliorum et Epistolae Decretales ac Constitutiones Summorum Pontificium* (12 vols., Parisiis, 1714-1715), II, 1042 (hereafter cited Hardouin); Vaison (529), can. 2—*op. cit.*, II, 1105; Trullo (692), cann. 19, 20, 64—*op. cit.*, II, 1670-1672.

and translation. The apostolic life of the monastic Orders consisted in observing the evangelical counsels after the example of the Apostles. But aside from a few extraordinary occasions and by way of exception, such as the preaching of the Crusades, neither the Benedictines nor the Cistercians were permitted by their Rule to engage in activities outside of the cloister.

St. Columban (ca. 543-615) and some few Benedictines of the various branches of the Benedictine Order devoted themselves to evangelizing parts of Europe, but the Rule of St. Columban made no mention of preaching, such activity being undertaken and carried on solely on the personal initiative of the individual. In fact, the canon law of the time forbade monks to preach to the people outside of their own houses, unless they had special permission from the Holy See.[2]

Article 2. Rise of the Mendicant Orders

A. The Franciscans

In the year 1223, Pope Honorius III (1216-1227) approved a new religious Order.[3] Since its foundation in 1209, the members of this new Order tried to emulate the public life of Christ and His Apostles by going out on the streets and preaching to the multitudes. St. Francis of Assisi (1182-1226), from whom as its founder the Order obtained its popular name of Franciscan, made missionary

[2] The following *dictum* was widely held as a rule for monks: ". . . Monachus non *doctoris* habet, sed *plangentis, officium*. . . ."—S. Hieronymus, *Contra Vigilantium*, n. 15—*MPL*, XXIII, 367; Pope Alexander II (1061-1073) decreed: "Monachis quamvis religiosis, ad normam Sancti Benedicti intra claustrum morari praecipimus; vicos, castella, civitates peragrare prohibemus, et a populorum praedicatione omnino cessare censuimus. . . ."—*MPL*, CXVI, 363; Mills, "Preaching, the *Opus Franciscanum*"—*The Franciscan Educational Conference* (an annual report, Brookland, Washington, D. C.: Capuchin College, 1919—), IX (1927), 107-109.

[3] Bulla *Solet annuere*, 29 nov. 1223—*Bullarum Diplomatum et Privilegiorum Sanctorum Romanorum Pontificum Taurinensis Edito* (24 vols. et Appendix, Augustae Taurinorum, 1857-1872), III, 394-399 (hereafter cited *Bull. Rom. Taur.*).

work among Christians and among infidels the primary purpose of the new Order.

The Pope approved this purpose when he approved the Order, and he stated that all the disciples of St. Francis should be entitled to exercise the apostolate of preaching in the entire world, provided they received from their founder the due permission to preach. This preaching activity was something entirely new, being neither known nor practiced by the older Orders. The Franciscans soon spread all over Italy and the other countries of Europe. They were popular missionaries in the truest sense of the word. They went from town to town preaching to the people everywhere, in the public places as well as in the churches.[4]

B. The Dominicans

Shortly after the foundation of the Franciscans, St. Dominic (1170-1221), in 1215, founded the Order of Preachers, commonly called the Dominicans. The Order was approved by Pope Honorius III (1216-1227) in 1216.[5] It also was a Mendicant Order, and its purpose was to refute heresy and to renew Christian fervor among the people by preaching. The preaching privileges which were given to the Dominicans were similar to those later given to the Franciscans, and the two Orders opened an era of apostolic activity in the home missions which has seldom been surpassed.

Naturally, the new impetus in preaching on the part of the Mendicant Orders occasioned opposition on the side of the bishops and the secular clergy because of the broad powers that had been granted. Bishops and pastors had long been suspicious and resentful of the wandering missionaries who entered the territories subject to their care and preached to the people, for many of these missionaries claimed exemption from the jurisdiction of the bishops. These preaching privileges were somewhat modified by Pope Boniface VIII (1294-1303) in the Bull *Super cathedram* in the year 1300.[6]

[4] Schroeder, "Missions, parochial,"—*CE,* X, 393; Strayer-Munro, *The Middle Ages* (New York: D. Appleton-Century, 1928), p. 308.

[5] Bulla *Religiosam vitam,* 22 dec. 1216—*Bull. Rom. Taur.,* III, 309-311.

[6] c. 2, *de sepulturis,* III, 7, in Clem.

This bull reaffirmed the right of the Dominicans and Franciscans to preach in the open squares and in their own places, but added that they should refrain from doing so when the bishop himself desired to preach or to have another preach in his presence. Bishops were requested by the Holy Father to treat the friars with consideration. The instructions of Boniface VIII were partially annulled by Benedict XI (1303-1304),[7] but were renewed by Clement V (1305-1314),[8] and were extended by John XXII (1316-1334)[9] to the Hermits of St. Augustine and to the Carmelites. The approval and co-operation of the Holy See in the activities of the Mendicant Orders were largely responsible for the development of preaching in general and of the sacred missions in particular.[10]

Article 3. Use of Missionary Preaching to Check the Reformation

A. The Bishops and the Secular Clergy

Once the Protestant revolt was in full sway, endeavors were made by the Pope, by the bishops, and by the secular clergy to check its spread. The means used were preaching and the use of a series of doctrinal instructions, similar to the present day sacred missions. The Popes and the various councils condemned not only those who were preaching heresy after having apostatized from the Church, but also those who remained in the Church and were guilty of

[7] C. 1, *de privilegiis,* V, 7, in Extravag. com.

[8] C. 2, *de sepulturis,* III, 7, in Clem.

[9] Cap. un., *de iudiciis,* II, 1, in Extravag. com.

[10] ". . . Il est bien difficile de dire exactement à quelle époque remontent les missions. Peut-être foundrait-il en charcher l'origine dans les prédications qu'avec l'assentiment et les encouragements des Evêques et du Saint-Siège, saint Dominique et saint François d'Assise organiserent dans une grande partie de l'Europe, au XIIIe siècle, et que continuèrent ensuite non seulement les Frères Prêcheurs et Mineurs, mais aussi d'autres religieux qui vinrent plus tard. Nous disons l'orgine, cur nous n'oserions pas affirmer que ces premieres prédications des fils de saint Dominique et de saint François d'Assise, qui firent tant de bien realisèrent des le début le programme de la Mission telle qu'on devait l'entendre quelques siècles apres. . . ."—Couly, "Des Missions,"—*Le Canoniste* (*Le Canoniste Contemporain,* Paris, 1878-1922, *Le Canoniste,* Paris, 1924-1926), XLVI (1924), 288-289.

frivolous or unorthodox preaching.[11] Preachers were urged to concentrate on the fundamental doctrines of the Church, and thus by simplicity and by the sheer weight of their teaching they were to refute the Protestants who had made oratory their main weapon in spreading their errors.[12]

Great bishops, such as St. Charles Borromeo (1538-1584) in Milan, organized their priests, reformed preaching, and achieved wonders in combating heresy. The *Confraternity of Christian Doctrine* was established in 1562 at Rome, was approved by Pope St. Pius V (1566-1572) in 1571,[13] and was endowed with indulgences by Pope Paul V (1605-1621) in 1607.[14] This confraternity, which did much to systematize the teaching of religion, was developed to a large extent by the secular clergy and their bishops, who began to realize that multitudes had fallen away from the Faith through ignorance of their religion. This orderly presentation of the doctrines of the Catholic religion was to have a considerable influence upon the later development of sacred missions.

B. The Various Religious Clergy

Especially noteworthy in fighting the spread of the errors of Protestantism was the newly-founded Society of Jesus.[15] The Jesuits fought error by preaching the truth. Led by their founder, St.

[11] Lateran V (1516), Leo X (1513-1521), bulla *Supernae maiestatis praesidio,* 19 dec. 1516—*Codicis Iuris Canonici Fontes,* cura Emi Petri Card. Gasparri editi (9 vols., Romae [postea Civitate Vaticanae]: Typis Polyglottis Vaticanis, 1923-1939, Vols. VII, VIII, IX, ed. cura et studio Emi Iustiniani Card. Serédi), n. 71 (hereafter cited *Fontes*); Trier II (1549), can. 2—Mansi, *Sacrorum Conciliorum Nova et Amplissima Collectio* (53 vols. in 59, Parisiis, Arnhem et Leipzig, 1901-1927), XXXII, 1441 (hereafter cited Mansi); Narbonne (1551), can. 31, 37—*op. cit.*, X, 453.

[12] Baudrillart, *The Catholic Church, the Renaissance and Protestantism* (translated by Mrs. Philip Gibbs, New York: Benziger Bros., 1908), pp. 134-140; Schmidlin, *Catholic Mission History,* pp. 251-274; Pollen, "Counter-Reformation," *CE,* IV, 441-445.

[13] Const. *Ex debito,* 6 oct. 1571—*Fontes,* n. 141.

[14] Bulla *Ex credito Nobis,* 9 nov. 1607,—*Bull. Rom. Taur.,* XI, 442-451.

[15] Paulus III (1534-1549), bulla *Regimini militantis Ecclesiae,* 27 sept. 1540—*Bull. Rom. Taur.,* VI, 303-306.

Ignatius Loyola (1491-1556), and using his famous *Exercises,* they brought back many to the Faith.

Other religious were active in the fight against the Protestant Reformation. The most prominent among these were the Capuchins, who were founded as a reformed branch of the Franciscans in 1525 and were approved by the Holy See in 1528.[16]

The Dominicans also had much to do with combating the Reformation and in developing the popular style of preaching. Before the Reformation, in the fourteenth century, they had Tauler (1300-1361) and Blessed Henry Suso (1295-1366), in the fifteenth, St. Vincent Ferrer (1350-1419) and Savonarola (1452-1498), and at the time of the Reformation, Louis of Granada (1505-1588). Famous popular missionaries of the Franciscan Order who were active during this period were Saints Bernadine of Sienna (1380-1444), John Capistrano (1386-1456), and Peter of Alcantara (1499-1562). In 1524, at Rome, the *Congregation of Clerks Regular,* members of whom are popularly known as the *Theatine Fathers,* was founded by St. Cajetan (1480-1547). The particular purpose of these religious was to campaign against the errors of the Reformation by preaching and catechizing among the people.[17]

Article 4. Attitude of Holy See on Popular Missionary Preaching

A. Legislation of the Council of Trent

The Council of Trent (1545-1563), although not treating missionary preaching specifically, nevertheless passed a number of decrees on preaching which had considerable effect on the development of missions. The Fifth Session, June 17, 1546, reaffirmed the instructions of previous councils concerning the obligation of preaching on the part of bishops. They were to preach either personally or through competent substitutes. Parish priests and others having

[16] Clemens VII (1523-1534), bulla *Religionis zelus,* 3 iul. 1528—*Bull. Rom. Taur.,* VI, 113-115.

[17] Clemens VII, bulla *Exponi nobis,* 24 iun. 1524—*Bull. Rom. Taur.,* VI, 73-74.

the care of souls were also bound to see that the faithful entrusted to their care were properly instructed. Failure to fulfill this duty made them liable to censures and other penalties according to the discretion of the ordinary.[18]

The purpose of the Fifth and Twenty-second Sessions of the Council of Trent was to reaffirm the pastoral duty of preaching, and the reform chapters of these sessions sought to correct various pulpit abuses and to insist upon the necessity of preaching in order to fight heresy. The Council of Trent, in these sessions, sought also to put an end to the centuries-old dispute between regulars and bishops about the right of preaching. The necessity of the canonical mission for preaching was established by the Council of Trent in settlement of this question. Regulars needed the approval of their superiors for preaching, and if they preached elsewhere than in their own churches they needed the approval also of the local ordinary.[19]

The Twenty-third Session of the Council of Trent is of interest because of its insistence upon definite boundaries for parishes, and in view of the command laid upon pastors correspondingly to provide for their people by offering Mass, by administering the sacraments, by doing good works, by preaching to them, and by seeing that they were properly instructed in their Faith. The pattern of their obligations thus followed that which had been established by the Council of Trent for bishops.[20]

Regulations were made also concerning the manner of preaching and the quality of the sermon material. Preachers were warned against preaching doubtful things for certain, and the practice of using undignified jokes and stories was severely reprimanded.[21]

The Twenty-fourth Session approved the *Catechism of the Council of Trent,* also called the *Roman Catechism.* This work was important because it has served as a guide for all preachers down

[18] Sess. V, *de ref.,* c. 2; Schroeder, *Canons and Decrees of the Council of Trent* (St. Louis: Herder, 1941), pp. 26-30; McVann, pp. 24-26.

[19] Sess. V, *de ref.,* c. 2; sess. XXII, *de ref.,* c. 4.

[20] Sess. XXIII, *de ref.,* c. 1; Schroeder, *Canons and Decrees of the Council of Trent,* pp. 165-170.

[21] Sess. XXIV, *de ref.,* c. 4.

to the present day. It was drawn up for the use of pastors in their instructions, and was thoroughly examined by theologians with a view to promoting absolute orthodoxy of doctrine.[22]

B. Approval of Popular Missionary Preaching

Approval of missions as such by the Holy See was not given until the eighteenth century, but the splendid work being done by the popular missionaries was acknowledged long before that time. Fearing that some of the strict regulations of the Council of Trent would interfere with the efforts of the religious Orders in developing this work, Pope St. Pius V (1566-1572) set aside the regulations of the Twenty-fourth Session of the Council of Trent, which had decreed that a regular could not preach without asking the bishop's blessing or proceed against the bishop's objections. The Pope listed twenty-six hindrances that bishops were putting in the way of the good works and rights of the Mendicant Orders. He charged that some bishops refused altogether to grant the permission to preach, regardless of the recommendation of superiors. Others were giving their permission only after the payment of a tax. The Pope withdrew the Mendicants from this provision of the Council of Trent. Thereafter they could preach in their own churches without reference to the bishop.[23] Later Popes restored the rigor of the Tridentine law relative to the Mendicant Orders and other regulars.[24]

In emphasizing the power of the ordinary to control preaching within his diocese, the Holy See merely wished to stop bickering

[22] Sess. XXIV, *de ref.*, c. 2; McHugh-Callan, *Catechism of the Council of Trent for Parish Priests* (New York: Wagner, 1923), pp. 23-25.

[23] Const. *Etsi mendicantium,* 16 maii 1567—*Fontes,* n. 121; const. *Ex supernae,* 16 aug. 1567—*op. cit.,* n. 122; const. *Ad hoc,* 23 sept. 1567—*Bull. Rom. Taur.,* VII, 587-595.

[24] Gregorius XIII, const. *In tanta,* 1 mart. 1573—*Bull. Rom. Taur.,* VIII, 39-41; S.C.C., *Elboren.,* 24 iul. 1595—*Fontes,* n. 2290; S.C.C., *Andrien.,* 23 ian. 1608—*op. cit.,* n. 2369; Gregorius XV, const. *Inscrutabili,* 5 febr. 1622, §§ 3, 6—*op. cit.,* n. 199; Clemens X, const. *Superna,* 21 iun. 1670, §§ 1-3—*op. cit.,* n. 246; Benedictus XIII, const. *Pretiosus,* 25 maii 1727—*Bull. Rom. Taur.,* XXII, 522-554; Benedictus XIV, const. *Ad militantis,* 30 mart. 1742—*Fontes,* n. 326.

and to preserve discipline. Far from discouraging the work of the popular missionaries, the various Popes of this period encouraged it and desired that this type of preaching be held in all parishes, whether secular or regular.[25]

[25] S.C. Ep. et Reg., *Maceraten.*, 7 mart. 1579—*Fontes,* n. 1353; S.C. Ep. et Reg., *Senen.*, 23 iul. 1694—*op. cit.*, n. 1816.

CHAPTER III

FROM THE SEVENTEENTH TO THE NINETEENTH CENTURY

ARTICLE 1. THE IMMEDIATE ANTECEDENTS OF SACRED MISSIONS

THE proximate occasion for the rise of missions seems to have been the emphasis on preaching during the Counter-Reformation in the sixteenth century. Protestantism had replaced the altar with the pulpit. While the Catholic Church could never sacrifice the center of its dogma and devotion in favor of preaching, nevertheless the Church authorities realized that the best way to fight heresy is to preach the truth. Consequently doctrinal preaching was strongly encouraged, and there were founded new religious societies whose specific purpose it was to fight heresy by preaching the orthodox doctrines.[1]

A. The Public Exercises of St. Ignatius Loyola

One of the most famous of the societies which fought the Reformation, as has already been mentioned, was the Society of Jesus, founded by St. Ignatius Loyola in 1534 and approved in 1540 by Pope Paul III.[2] The Jesuits soon spread over all of Europe, and combated heresy wherever they found it. One of their principal weapons in bringing back many to the Faith was the public presentation of the *Exercises of St. Ignatius.* These exercises consisted of instructions, admonitions, warnings, prayers, meditations, examination of conscience, and other practices. Pope Paul III gave his approval to the practice of holding the *Exercises of St. Ignatius* in public.[3]

[1] Couly, "Des Missions,"—*Le Canoniste,* XLVI (1924), 288-290.

[2] Const. *Regimini militantis Ecclesiae,* 27 sept. 1540—*Bull. Rom. Taur.,* VI, 303-306.

[3] Const. *Licet debitum,* 18 oct. 1549—*Bull. Rom. Taur.,* VI, 394-401.

Some of the great Jesuit preachers during this period were St. Peter Canisius (1521-1591), who became known as the *malleus haereticorum,* and St. John Francis Regis (1597-1640), who was a famous social worker as well as an outstanding missionary.[4] In Italy, the Jesuit preacher, Paul Segneri (1624-1694), attracted great crowds, and St. Francis di Geronimo (1642-1716) established at Naples the *Oratorio delle Missioni* in order to provide lay helpers who would bring people to the missions.[5]

B. The Capuchin Missions

The Capuchins played a very important part in the history of the people's mission. Eusebius of Merlon (+1618) and his Capuchin *confrères* traveled through much of Europe, preaching to the people and catechizing. This type of preaching gradually became systematized with the development of definite sermon topics and a regular plan of procedure before the end of the sixteenth century.[6]

The missionary work of the Capuchins was not confined to any particular country in Europe. Missions were given by them in Italy under the leadership of John of Ferno (+1556), Girolamo of Narni (+1632), and Francis of Negro (+1650). A distinctive feature of the Capuchin missions in Italy was the opening or closing of the mission with the *Forty Hours' Devotion.* This devotion began at Milan about the year 1534, and it soon spread into other cities of Italy. It has not been definitely settled who started this devotion, but it subsequently received the approval of several Popes.[7]

[4] Daubenton, *La vie du B. Jean François Regis* (Paris, 1716), p. 73.

[5] Bach (ed.), *Histoire de S. François de Geronimo* (Metz, 1851), p. 30. For a full treatment of the part played by the Jesuits in the Counter-Reformation confer Ridley, *The Jesuits, a Study in Counter-Reformation* (London: Secker and Warburg, 1938).

[6] Rocco da Cesinale, *Storia delle Missioni dei Cappuccini* (3 vols., Paris, 1867-1873), I, 166-172; Zawart, "History of Franciscan Preaching and Preachers"—*Franciscan Educational Conference,* IX (1927), 283-387.

[7] E.g., Paulus III, bulla *Dominus Noster,* 30 nov. 1537—*Bull. Rom. Taur.,* VI, 275-280; Clemens VIII, bulla *Graves et diuturnae,* 25 nov. 1592—*op. cit.,* IX, 644-647; cf. Zawart, "History of Franciscan Preaching and Preachers"—*Franciscan Educational Conference,* IX (1927), 392; for a complete treat-

Missions were given by the Capuchins throughout France, but particularly in the Provinces of Picardy, Provence, Normandy, and Languedoc. The primitive development of missions in France by the Capuchins apparently had no connection with the later development of sacred missions by the Vincentians. It is difficult to determine whether the one influenced the other. Some of the more prominent Capuchin missionaries in France included Jerome of Laurens (+1617), Valentine of Nantes (+1614), and Francis of Toulouse (+1678).[8] Religious processions and pilgrimages to the ancient shrines were characteristic of the early Capuchin missions in France. By 1613 the Capuchin missionaries had spread into almost every province of France. Their work was approved by King Louis XIII (1610-1643) and by many of the French bishops.[9]

The first attempts at the organization and systematization of popular missions were made by Joseph of Tremblay, O.F.M.Cap. (1577-1638), known principally as the friend and counsellor of Cardinal Richelieu (1585-1642). Under the leadership of Père Joseph, mission houses were established in Poitou, Niort, Saint-Maxence, and Loudon. There was begun an organized missionary enterprise which was composed of specially chosen and trained friars. In 1608 there were obtained from Pope Paul V, along with faculties to absolve and to reconcile heretics to the Church, certain other concessions for facilitating their missionary endeavors.[10] These preachers were given missionary faculties, and were dependent on

ment of the controversy over the origin of the *Forty Hours' Devotion*, confer Bergamaschi, *Dell' Origine delle SS. Quarantore* (Cremona, 1897).

[8] Francis of Toulouse is of special interest because he wrote *Le Missionaire Parfait* (2 vols., Paris, 1662), which was the first work to treat of parochial missions in detail; *Franciscan Educational Conference*, IX (1927), 481.

[9] Henry III (1612-1652), Bishop of Metz and Cardinal of Lorraine, spoke about the spread of the Capuchin missions in a letter to the governor of Rheims: ". . . not in one place but in divers provinces and cities of the kingdom they labour with ardent zeal and charity to bring about the salvation of the souls of the faithful; and by instructions and persuasive sermons, as well as by the example of their holy work, have so succeeded that the fruits of their harvest daily become manifest to all eyes. . . ."—*Analecta Ordinis Minorum Capuccinorum*, V, 59, quoted in Cuthbert, *The Capuchins* (3 vols., Longmans, Green & Co., 1929), II, 257-261.

[10] Bulla *Ecclesiae militantis*, 15 oct. 1608—*Bull. Rom. Taur.*, XI, 552-553.

the Sacred Congregation of the Holy Office, so that the missionaries if once sent could not be recalled without the permission of the Congregation; in other words, they were "apostolic missionaries," like the missionaries sent to the foreign missions.[11]

The Capuchins, under the leadership of Cherubim de Maurienne (+1610) and with the encouragement of St. Francis de Sales (1567-1622), the Bishop of Geneva, gave missions alongside of the Jesuits in Switzerland. Spain also witnessed their missionary activity under the Venerable Joseph of Carabantes (+1694), and missions were given throughout Austria, Germany, and the Netherlands under the leadership of St. Lorenzo of Brindisi (1559-1619) and his *confrères*.[12] Under the direction of Francis Nugent (+1635), missions were given secretly by the Capuchins and the Jesuits throughout England, Scotland, and Ireland, until the penal laws made the work absolutely prohibitive.[13]

C. *The Missionary Activity of Other Religious*

The other branches of the Franciscan family, the Dominicans, and the various religious and secular clergy also partook in the gradual development of sacred missions throughout Europe. The *Oratorians,* founded in 1575 by St. Philip Neri (1515-1595), and the *Eudists,* founded by St. John Eudes (1601-1680) in 1643, were quasi-religious societies and were active in the parochial mission field. In 1612 the Oratorians were given permission by Pope Paul V (1605-1621) to give public exercises.[14] St. John Eudes set the example for his society, for it is reported that he gave 110 missions during his lifetime.[15]

Article 2. Sacred Missions Properly So Called

The Jesuits and Capuchins, during the sixteenth and early seventeenth centuries, were the first to give missions, but planned sacred

[11] Cuthbert, *The Capuchins,* II, 263-264.

[12] Cuthbert, *op. cit.,* II, 285-361.

[13] Cuthbert, *op. cit.,* II, 329-340.

[14] Paulus V, bulla *Christifidelium,* 24 febr. 1612—*Bull. Rom. Taur.,* XII, 36-57.

[15] De Montzey, *Father Eudes, Apostolic Missionary and His Foundations* (Boston: Patrick Donohoe, 1874), pp. 204-224.

missions, as they are known today, were not developed until the middle of the seventeenth century. The beginning of the seventeenth century was a period of religious disintegration in France as in other European countries, and the need of the faithful for proper instruction had become increasingly apparent. The clergy, too few in numbers and poorly trained, could do little to remedy the situation. As so often happens in history, the right man appeared to supply the need. That man was the great Saint Vincent de Paul (1581-1660).

A. Development by St. Vincent de Paul and the Vincentians

Vincent de Paul was ordained in Dax, France, in 1600. After an adventurous and rather varied experience during the early years of his priesthood, he obtained a position as chaplain at the Chateau de Folleville in Picardy with the family of Emmanuel de Gondy, Count de Joigny, General of the Galleys.[16]

On January 25, 1617, a remarkable sermon was preached by St. Vincent de Paul in the village church of Folleville. It was a simple sermon on the benefits of making a good general confession, but it produced astonishing results. So many of the villagers desired to go to confession that it was necessary to obtain the aid of two Jesuits from a nearby village. Impressed by this incident, Madame de Gondy asked Vincent to give regular courses of instruction for the villagers near her estates. These courses were given the name of missions and soon became very popular.[17]

In 1625, with the encouragement of Madame de Gondy and the approval of her brother-in-law, Jean François de Gondy, Archbishop of Paris (1622-1654), Vincent with a few secular priests began giving missions in the rural districts near Paris. He preached a mission on the galleys of Bordeaux in the same year that he began this work among the country people.[18]

[16] *Saint Vincent de Paul, Correspondence, Entretiens, Documents* (40 vols. in 14, Paris, 1920-1925), XI, 329, XII, 43; Coste, *Monsieur Vincent, le grand saint du grand siècle* (3 vols., Paris: Desclé, 1931), I, 43-91 (hereafter cited Coste).

[17] Coste, I, 88-91.

[18] Coste, I, 140-155, 171-187.

The ownership and all the rights of an old college in Paris, called "des Bons Enfants," were turned over to Vincent de Paul by Archbishop de Gondy of Paris. On April 24, 1626, the same Archbishop gave his official approval to Vincent de Paul's newly-formed *Congregation of the Fathers of the Mission.* On January 7, 1632, the house of St. Lazare in Paris was given to the Congregation, and it soon became the headquarters from which the members obtained the popular name of Lazarists.[19]

St. Vincent de Paul had first applied to Rome for approval of his Congregation in 1625, but Pope Urban VIII (1623-1644) did not approve of such an undertaking at that time. It was the desire of Vincent to have a community of secular priests who would not have the status of religious with public vows, but who would take private vows and be bound closely together. This was a new concept, and it was not until January 12, 1632, that the Pope approved the Congregation.[20]

The missions given by St. Vincent de Paul and his companions were quite similar to present-day missions. One feature which Vincent de Paul insisted upon was that of giving all missions gratuitously, and he would not agree to the establishment of a mission house unless it had a sufficient foundation so that the missions might be given without charge of any kind. These missions were given over all of France, and ranged from the rural districts to the suburbs of Paris, and even to the court of King Louis XIII (1610-1643), where, at the king's insistence, Vincent gave a mission at St. Germain-en-Laye near Paris in 1638. From 1652 to 1660 more than 700 missions were given from the house of St. Lazare alone.[21]

It is important to notice, in following the rise of the obligation of holding sacred missions, that St. Vincent de Paul together with

[19] Coste, I, 190-207.

[20] Bulla *Salvatoris Nostri—Bull. Rom. Taur.*, XIV, 272-273.

[21] Randolph, "Congregation of Priests of the Mission," *CE*, X, 360. St. Vincent de Paul himself summed up his admiration for the parochial mission in the following words: ". . . O saint et divin exercice, qui donne de l'honneur a l'Eglise, de la doctrine aux pauvres ignorants et une grande consolation a ceux qui les enseignent! Plut a mon Dieu que ceux que Dieu a appeles a l'etat ecclesiastique voulussent imiter la plupart de ceux qui travaillent dedans Paris. La France en serait mieux cultivee. . . ."—Coste, III, 29.

his friend, the Venerable Jean Jacques Olier (1608-1657), founder of the Sulpicians, was largely responsible for the reform of the clergy in France and for the training of ecclesiastical students. It is certain that the utility of sacred missions received due emphasis in the conferences given to those who were to become the clergy and hierarchy of France. Upon the recommendation of St. Vincent de Paul, many bishops were chosen from the ranks of those who attended his famous "Tuesday" conferences. Cardinals Richelieu, de Gondy, and La Retz (1614-1679), and other prominent French prelates, turned instinctively to St. Vincent for advice when submitting names for appointment to vacant sees.[22]

B. Organization by St. Alphonsus Liguori and the Redemptorists

St. Alphonsus Liguori (1696-1787) was ordained to the priesthood on December 21, 1726. For six years he gave missions in and around Naples as a member of an association of missionary secular priests called the *Neapolitan Propaganda.* On November 9, 1732, St. Alphonsus founded a society of missionary priests at Scala, Naples, known as the *Congregation of the Most Holy Redeemer,* for the purpose of laboring among the neglected country people in the neighborhood of Naples. Their work soon spread over all the states which now make up the country of Italy. Pope Benedict XIV (1740-1758) canonically approved the work of the Redemptorists by means of an Apostolic Letter issued in 1749.[23]

St. Alphonsus owed much for the success of his endeavors to the co-operation of the Archbishop of Naples, Giuseppe Cardinal Spinelli (1734-1754), who became known as the patron of sacred missions. This prelate urged all those having the care of souls in his diocese to partake in general missions to be held in all the parishes of the city at a given time.[24]

Largely through the efforts of the Redemptorist missionary, St. Clement Mary Hofbauer (1751-1821), sacred missions were given

[22] Coste, III, 100-125.

[23] *Nos bene scimus,* 25 febr. 1749, quoted in Berthé, *Saint Alphonse de Liguori* (2 vols., Paris, 1907), I, 383.

[24] *Istruzione per li Missionari deputati anno 1741,* cited by Berthé, *op. cit.,* I, 222-225.

in Austria, Germany, and Poland. The principal mission house for Poland was that of St. Benno, which was often called a continuous mission because of the activity and zeal manifested there.[25]

A novel characteristic in sacred missions was introduced by the Redemptorists. After having given the regular mission, they returned after four or five months and preached a shorter mission or renewal. This became a regular procedure in Redemptorist missions. Like the Vincentians before them, the Redemptorists at first gave their missions entirely *gratis*.[26] St. Alphonsus gave minute instructions on how missions were to be conducted.[27]

Although not mentioning any specific obligation of giving missions in the parish, St. Alphonsus said that a good pastor would not let four or five years go without a mission.[28] St. Alphonsus urged missionaries not to interfere with the internal affairs of the parish

[25] Stebbing, *The Redemptorists* (New York: Benziger Bros., 1924), p. 58.

[26] Stebbing *op. cit.*, pp. 3, 5.

[27] The daily schedule for the mission was outlined: (1) Meditation; (2) Christian Doctrine or Catechism; (3) Rosary; (4) Sermon; (5) Discipline for the men (four or five times during the mission, and on the last night the ceremony of the trailing of the tongue; (6) Sermon of the Blessing (on the last day of the mission); (7) General Communion (on the last day of the mission); and (8) Exercises of the Devout Life (on the last three days of the mission). The missions should last at least ten or twelve days. Some of the features of the early Redemptorist missions, such as the ceremony of the trailing of the tongue, may appear strange to those who are accustomed to modern sacred missions. St. Alphonsus describes this impressive ceremony as follows: ". . . on the last evening [of the mission], instead of the discipline, it is customary to trail the tongue on the ground, an exercise very useful for those that have the habit of blaspheming and of uttering immodest language. . . ."—*The Complete Ascetical Works of Saint Alphonsus de Liguori* (translated by Eugene Grimm, Centenary Edition, 24 vols., New York: Benziger Bros., 1887-1893), XV, 121-123.

[28] ". . . Cum in regione reperiuntur notabiles morum dissolutiones, quibus nullum occurrit remedium, parochus tenetur curare, ut missio eo adveniat (ille parochus, qui missionem non curat, suspicionem ingerit suorum morum; boni enim parochi non praetermittunt quarto aut quinto quoque anno Missionem arcessere). . . ."—*Homo Apostolicus* (Augustae Taurinorum: Marietti, 1876), Tract VII, n. 31, p. 144; Wernz, *Ius Decretalium* (2. ed., 6 vols., Romae: Prati, 1906-1913), III, 59.

in which they preached, and he gave rules for their conduct when on missions.[29]

In a letter, written for the information of bishops on the utility of sacred missions, St. Alphonsus mentioned the principal objections which were commonly advanced against the holding of sacred missions, but he offered a capable refutation.[30] St. Alphonsus pointed

[29] (1) No one shall go on missions by himself, there should be at least two missionaries;

(2) They shall always travel to the missions on foot;

(3) Having reached their destination, the time for the exercises should be set. Missions should not be given in the Summer. Missioners should take seven hours of sleep in Winter, and six and a half hours of sleep in the Spring, and about one hour of rest during the day;

(4) Missioners should keep to the confessionals to which they have been assigned;

(5) They should avoid familiarity and useless conversation;

(6) They should make a half hour's meditation twice a day;

(7) Silence should be kept at the table while the missioners eat; and

(8) In regard to the expenses of the mission, nothing should ever be asked unless it be for food, house, beds, and other necessities.—*The Complete Ascetical Works of Saint Alphonsus,* XV, 338-342.

[30] The five main objections mentioned by St. Alphonsus were:

(1) The fruit of missions is only temporary;

(2) The consciences of many are disturbed by scruples which are excited by the sermons;

(3) The exercises of the mission generally end at night and are therefore a cause of much scandal;

(4) Some imprudent missionaries preach from the pulpit against the sins which they hear in the confessional, and excite in the people a hatred for confession; and

(5) Missions being repeated every three years are too frequent, and therefore produce little or no impression on the people.

In answering these objections St. Alphonsus stressed his opinion of the great value of sacred missions: ". . . It is certain that the conversion of sinners is the greatest benefit that God can bestow upon man; but the conversion of sinners is precisely the end of missions, for by the instructions and sermons of the missions they are convinced of the malice of sin, of the importance of salvation and of the goodness of God, and thus their hearts are changed, the bonds of vicious habits are broken and they begin to live like Christians. . . . I hold for certain that, if among all those who have attended the mission sermons, anyone die within a year after the missions, he will scarcely be lost. . . ."—*op. cit.,* XV, 73-75.

out that the entire good work of sacred missions should not be condemned because of the weaknesses manifested by some preachers. Furthermore, he declared that some of the things mentioned, such as the arousing of the consciences of the people, were blessings rather than evils.

C. Popularization by St. Leonard of Port Maurice and Others

St. Leonard Casanova (1676-1751), called Leonard of Port Maurice because of his birthplace in what is now Italy, was destined to be one day officially declared the patron of missions among Catholics.[31] St. Leonard belonged to the *Riformella,* which was an offshoot of the *Reformati* branch of the Franciscan Order. He received the habit in 1697, and was ordained to the priesthood in 1704. Soon afterwards Leonard was sent to the monastery of Monte alle Croci, near Florence, and there he began his work of giving missions to the people. Great austerities and severe penances were practiced by St. Leonard and his companions during their missions. In 1720 he held missions in central and southern Italy, and in 1744 on the Island of Corsica. His fame became widespread, and he was called to Rome at various times by Popes Clement XII (1730-1740) and Benedict XIV (1740-1758). A *Diary* of St. Leonard's missions was written by Fra Diego of Florence (+1767), which proved a valuable help for later missionaries.[32]

The Congregation of Discalced Clerks of the Most Holy Cross and Passion of Our Lord Jesus Christ, the members of which are better known as the *Passionists,* was founded by St. Paul of the Cross (1694-1775) at Castellazzo, Italy. Oral permission was obtained in 1725 from Pope Benedict XIII (1724-1730) to found a congregation, and the rules of the institute were approved in an Apostolic Rescript of Pope Benedict XIV on May 15, 1741,[33] and

[31] Pope Pius XI designated St. Leonard of Port Maurice as the patron of missions among Catholics on March 17, 1923, in an Apostolic Letter—*Acta Apostolicae Sedis* (Romae, 1909—), XV (1923), 196 (hereafter cited *AAS*).

[32] Cf. Di Ormea, *Vita del B. Leonardo da Porto Maurizio* (Romae, 1851); *Franciscan Educational Conference,* IX (1927), 522-524; Bihl, "Leonard of Port Maurice," *CE,* IX, 178-179.

[33] *Ne igitur—Bullarium Benedicti XIV* (4 vols., Romae: Typis Sacrae

confirmed by Pope Clement XIV (1769-1774) [84] and again by Pope Pius VI (1775-1799).[85]

The Passionists made the work of sacred missions an important part of their apostolic endeavors. They gave missions in cities and small towns throughout the Italian states, and by the end of the eighteenth century they had twelve retreat houses for their missionaries scattered at various places in the country. A characteristic feature of their missions was the emphasis placed on instructions about the Passion of Our Lord.[86]

The Holy Ghost Fathers, founded in 1703 by Claude François Poullart des Places (1679-1709) in Paris, France, and the *Missionaries of the Company of Mary,* founded by St. Louis Grignion de Montfort (1673-1716) in 1715, also were active in parochial missionary work during the eighteenth century, particularly in France. The *Montfortists,* although few in number, gave over 430 missions, most of which lasted a month, between the years 1718 and 1781.[87]

Article 3. Legislation on Sacred Missions

A. The Holy See

As missions gradually developed, they attracted the attention and approval of the Holy See. This approval was first manifested indirectly by the approbation given to the constitutions and work of such religious as the Capuchins and Vincentians, who made the giving of sacred missions one of their principal occupations. The Holy See encouraged their efforts and resisted attempts to curtail

Congregationis de Propaganda Fide, 1746-1763), II, 58 (hereafter cited *Bull. Benedicti XIV*).

[84] Bulla *Salvatoris Domini Nostri Iesu Christo,* 15 nov. 1769—*Bullarii Romani Continuatio* (edita ab A. Barberi, A. Spetia et R. Segreti, 20 vols., Romae, 1835-1857), IV, 98-119 (hereafter cited *Bull. Rom. Cont.*).

[85] Bulla *Praeclara virtutum,* 17 oct. 1775,—*op. cit.,* V, 155-158.

[86] For a more complete account of the history and missionary activity of the Passionists confer Ward, *Passionists* (New York: Benziger Bros., 1923).

[87] Bemelmans, "Missionaries of the Company of Mary," *CE,* IX, 749; Currier, *History of Religious Orders* (New York: Murphy and McCarthy, 1897), pp. 458-460; Pauvert, *Vie du venerable Louis Marie Grignion de Montfort* (Paris et Potiers, 1875).

their activities by those who looked with suspicion on their increasing popularity. In order, however, to remove causes for dissension between the missionaries and the bishops of the dioceses in which they preached, the necessity of the canonical mission was reaffirmed in all instructions which were issued on preaching. Pope Innocent XI (1676-1689) ruled also against the excesses of some sensational preachers, who were giving a bad name to the entire work of popular preaching. Theatrical and sentimental preaching, useless argumentation, and unorthodox doctrines and methods were strictly forbidden.[38]

A new Roman Congregation was established on June 22, 1622, for the supervision of all foreign missions. The seventeenth century soon became a fruitful one in missionary endeavor, and the Holy See encouraged this work by extending broad faculties to the apostolic missionaries who were working among Catholics and non-Catholics whether at home or abroad.[39]

Often sacred missions were given during the penitential seasons of Advent and of Lent, and they were thus closely related to the special Advent and Lent courses of sermons which had been ordered by the Council of Trent.[40] In many places it had long been the custom for lay patrons, universities, towns, and other groups to name the preachers for Advent and Lent. This led to many difficulties. Accordingly the Holy See, in various instructions, declared that the right of nomination could be retained by those who had it, but the nominations were subject to the approval of the local ordinary.[41]

[38] S.C.C., litt. encycl. 6 iul. 1680, n. 8—*Collectio Lacensis: Acta et Decreta Sacrorum Conciliorum Recentium* (7 vols., Friburgi-Brisgoviae: Herder, 1870-1892), I, 162 (hereafter cited *Coll. Lac.*).

[39] Gregorius XV, const. *Inscrutabili*, 22 iun. 1622, § 8—*Fontes*, n. 200.

[40] Sess. XXIV, *de ref.*, c. 4.

[41] S.C. Ep. et Reg., *Aprunita seu Theramen.*, 6 febr. 1615—Ferraris, *Prompta Bibliotheca Canonica, Iuridica, Moralis, Theologica, nec non Ascetica, Polemica, Rubristica, Historica* (8 vols., Romae, 1885-1892, Bucceroni, *Supplementum*, Romae, 1899), VI, s.v. *praedicare, praedicator*, p. 182, n. 43; S.C.C., *Narnien.*, 24 febr. 1625—Ferraris, *op. cit.*, VI, 182, n. 48; S.C.C., *Theanen.*, 14 apr. 1675—Ferraris, *loc. cit.*, S.C.C. *Sutrina*, 8 maii 1688—*Fontes*, n. 2906; Clemens X, const. *Superna*, 21 ian. 1670, §§ 1-3—*op. cit.*, n. 246.

The Holy See was desirous that all the faithful should receive the benefits offered by missions. Bishops were granted power to send missionaries into regular parishes without the consent of the superior if that proved necessary for ensuring the instruction of the faithful.[42]

The most important document on sacred missions ever issued was the Bull *Gravissimum* of Pope Benedict XIV, published on September 8, 1745.[43] It is important because it formed the basis for all of the succeeding legislation on sacred missions. In this bull the Pontiff pointed out first of all the serious duty of bishops and of pastors to provide thorough instruction for their poorly instructed flocks. Recalling his own experiences before he ascended the Chair of Peter, Benedict XIV stated that in his capacity of *Promotor Fidei* it had been one of his duties to examine the lives and virtues of those who were to be canonized. He was particularly impressed by the emphasis placed on sacred missions by such great saints as Cardinal Bellarmine (1542-1621), John Francis Regis, Vincent de Paul, and others. He had also served as secretary of the Sacred Congregation of the Council, in which office he had experienced close contact with the reports sent in by bishops on the success of sacred missions in their dioceses.[44]

As Chief Shepherd of the Sees of Ancona and later Bologna before he became Pope, Benedict XIV had the opportunity to come into direct contact with the work of sacred missions, and his admiration grew. Now as Pope he was determined that the universal Church should derive benefit from these spiritual exercises.[45]

[42] S.C. Ep. et Reg., *Senen.*, 23 iul. 1694—*Fontes,* n. 1816; Coronata, II, 274; Wernz, *Ius Decretalium,* III, 59.

[43] *Bull. Benedicti XIV,* I, 555-560.

[44] ". . . Itaque cum Nos ipsi Secretarii munere fungeremur, quoties in aliqua Dioecesi Missiones indictas fuisse relatum fuit, toties iussu Congregationis eiusdem, vel Summorum Pontificum, hoc concilium magnopere commendavimus in responsis, quae ad Episcopos fieri consueverunt, eosque incendere non praetermisimus, ut laudabiliter inceptum prosequerentur. Non semel etiam Episcopos redarguere iussi fuimus, qui pios Missionarios non accirent ut languentem, sicut ipsi offerebant, in Populo pietatem, et in Viris Ecclesiasticis disciplinam excitarent, et in utrisque peccandi licentiam cum scandalo iunctam coercerent. . . ."—*op. cit.,* I, 557, n. 7.

[45] ". . . Tandem Sacrarum Missionum utilitatem ac necessitatem Nos ipsi

The Pope urged also that missionaries be specially trained for this important work. They were to imitate the example of the great missionaries of the past and to seek the advice of successful contemporary missionaries. Extraordinary faculties to absolve apostates and heretics were extended to those giving sacred missions. Special praise was bestowed by the Pope on Cardinal Spinelli of Naples for the support given by him to the work of sacred missions. The Pope urged him to continue his support and to divide up the territory, so that the preaching bands would be more effective.[46]

A number of instructions issued by various Roman Congregations during the eighteenth century had passing reference to preaching and sacred missions, but next to the Bull *Gravissimum* of Benedict XIV the most important papal pronouncement was the Constitution *Auctorem fidei* of Pope Pius VI (1775-1799), which condemned the Synod of Pistoia. This synod, infamous for its errors, took place in 1786 at Pistoia in the Grand Duchy of Tuscany under the leadership of Scipio de' Ricci (1741-1810), the Bishop of Pistoia and Prato (1780-1790).

Members of this synod had become imbued with the Jansenistic spirit which had spread from France into Italy. The Jansenists were

compertam habuimus, quoties illas accivimus in Dioecesem Anconitanam, quo tempore Nobis commendata fuit, et quamdiu Bononiensem Ecclesiam Nosmet praesentes administravimus. Et nunc etiam curamus diligenter, ut eaedem Missiones quandoque indicantur ab eo, qui iuxta normam et consilia a Nobis perscripta, vices Nostras obtinuit. Tum plane agnovimus veritati consentaneum esse, quod Paulus Segneri Societatis Iesu, Concionatoris, Scriptoris, ac Missionarii laude clarissimus, scriptum reliquit, nempe: 'Missionum tempore tot concionatores merito nuncunpari posse, quot perculsi piis exercitationibus ad Poenitentiam inflammantur, suoque exemplo alios pertrahunt ad eandem virtutem exercendam. Ex illis autem Missionibus magis copiosum fructum dimanare, quibus maiori frequentia populus intersit, ea prorsus ratione, qua ignis augetur, si plures in unum locum carbones congerantur.'

"Suocirca neque novum, neque incertum, neque a Nobis excogitatum dici potest hoc remedium, quod Populi corruptelis corrigendis proponitur. Antiquum illud est, malis curandis aptissimum et fortasse unicum, quod tot Episcopi pietatis gloria insignes magna cum utilitate suis in Dioecesibus adhibuerunt, quod Nos ipsi toties experti sumus, et Vos etiam, qui procul dubio Populum Vobis commissum Sacris Missionibus aliquando recreastis. . . ."—*op. cit.*, I, 557, 9-10.

[46] *Loc. cit.*

bitterly opposed to sacred missions, because they believed they were unbecoming, and that they gave rise to a spirit of levity and disregard for religion. The Synod of Pistoia stated that sacred missions were an empty noise and that they did not leave any real effect upon the people.[47] The condemnation of this doctrine was important, for in effect it placed the stamp of approval by the Holy See on sacred missions, and thus silenced any who might still be opposed to the work.

B. Local Ecclesiastical Legislation

The first local legislation which mentioned missions was enacted by the Council of Bordeaux, France (1624). It advised that, along with the possession of other qualifications, preachers should be capable of directing the faithful in retreats and other spiritual exercises.[48] The obligation, of submitting to the ordinary for approval the names of the preachers for Advent and Lent, which frequently included mission preachers, was called to mind again by the Provincial Council of Benevento, Italy, in 1693.[49]

The year 1699 is a very important one in following the history of the obligation of holding sacred missions in parishes, for in that year was held the Provincial Council of Naples, which was the first council to enact legislation which made sacred missions obligatory. Missions had become quite successful in the Neapolitan area, and general missions were ordered by the Council to be held yearly and simultaneously in all the parishes in the cities, and particular missions were to be given in the towns and country places if at all possible.[50]

[47] The 65th Proposition of the Synod of Pistoia which stated: ". . . irregularem strepitum novarum institutionum, quae dictae sunt exercitia vel missiones, forte nunquam aut saltem perraro eo pertingere, ut absolutam conversionem operentur; et exteriores illos commotionis actus, qui apparuere, nil aliud fuisse quam transeuntia naturalis concussionis fulgura . . ." was condemned by Pope Pius VI as "'. . . temeraria, male, sonans, perniciosa, mori pie ac salutariter per Ecclesiam frequentato et in verbo Dei fundato iniuriosa. . . ." —Const. *Auctorem fidei,* 28 aug. 1794, ad LXV—*Fontes,* n. 475.

[48] Cap. XII—Hardouin, XI, 93-95.

[49] *Coll. Lac.,* I, 246.

[50] *Op. cit.,* I, 255.

An interesting development, recognized by the Provincial Council of Naples, was the practice in accordance with which the bishop sent special preachers to give sacred missions in parishes in order to prepare for the episcopal visitation. This custom was approved and heartily recommended by the Council.[51]

The Provincial Council which was held in Rome in 1725 urged preachers at sacred missions to preach the word of God, and not to indulge in human wisdom or unorthodox doctrine. They were to teach not only by their words but by their example as well. Regulars needed the approval both of their own superiors and of the bishops of the dioceses in which they were to preach.[52]

The Council of Avignon, France (1725), ruled that preachers from outside the diocese had to obtain their license to preach from the local bishop, who on the other hand was urged to favor sacred missions as a fruitful means of winning souls.[53] The Provincial Council of Tarragona, Spain (1727), urged that only those preachers who could speak the proper dialect were to be allowed to preach in a given district.[54]

In the near East, a Council of the Maronites, known as the Synod of Mount Lebanon, Syria (1736), stressed the necessity of the preacher's speaking in the language of the people. It urged, also, that missionaries, recruited either from the secular or from the religious clergy, were to be sent around to give missions, but they first had to obtain the permission of the local ordinary.[55]

C. Secular Law

Although specific laws against sacred missions were not common, the work was hampered through most of its history by inter-

51 ". . . Antequam Sanctam Visitationem ineat, Episcopus mittat operarios ante faciem suam in omnem civitatem et locum, quo fuerit ipse venturus, qui apostolicis missionibus parent viam Domini et rectas faciant semitas Dei Nostri. Praedicatores enim suos Dominus sequitur, et cum praedicatio praevenit, tunc ad mentis habitaculum Dominus venit. . . ."—*Coll. Lac.*, I, 217.

52 *Op. cit.*, I, 350.

53 Tit. III et IV—*op. cit.*, IV, 481.

54 *Op. cit.*, I, 326.

55 *Op. cit.*, II, 103-106.

ference from the secular power. First among the difficulties was that which confronted the missionaries shortly after the Reformation when they attempted to preach in countries governed by Protestant rulers. Generally they were forbidden to exercise their ministry in any way, so that they had to resort to the giving of the missions secretly.[56]

St. Vincent de Paul had difficulties with various local government officials who passed rules about the time and place where he could hold his sacred missions. Usually St. Vincent through his tact and patience was able to overcome such exasperating obstacles.[57]

The Redemptorists were continually in difficulties with the all too zealous government of the Kingdom of Naples. When St. Alphonsus Liguori tried to obtain the required royal *exsequatur*, the Neapolitan government placed so many restrictions on the rule and activities of the new congregation, that the Redemptorist houses in Naples were separated from the rest of the houses for a number of years during the eighteenth century. The Redemptorist missionary St. Clement Mary Hofbauer, was forbidden by the secular authorities to give sacred missions in Austria and the various German states.[58]

The French Revolution, of course, with its vehemently antireligious laws, brought almost complete disaster for the work of sacred missions in France, and it was a number of years before missions could effectively be resumed.[59]

[56] Cuthbert, *The Capuchins*, II, 285-340.

[57] Coste, I, 200-205.

[58] Stebbing, *The Redemptorists*, p. 58.

[59] For a more complete account of the effect of the French Revolution upon the Church in France, confer De la Gorce, *Histoire religieuse de la Revolution Francaise* (Paris, 1911).

CHAPTER IV

THE NINETEENTH CENTURY

ARTICLE 1. THE CONTINUED DEVELOPMENT OF SACRED MISSIONS

GREAT progress was made during the nineteenth century in the field of sacred missions. The work of new and old religious Orders, Congregations, and Societies, in addition to the efforts of the secular clergy, attracted the attention and approval of the Holy See and of the local councils which were held during this century.

A. The Bishops and the Secular Clergy

Many bishops and pastors were impressed by the progress made during the eighteenth century in the work of sacred missions, and also by the emphasis on this activity as manifested by several Popes. As a result, during the nineteenth century not only religious were invited into the dioceses and parishes to give these missions, but in many cases missionary bands of secular priests were established within the dioceses under the direction of their respective ordinaries.[1] These bands established mission headquarters, and began systematically to give missions throughout their dioceses. Their efforts achieved a great deal of success, and received praise in much of the legislation passed during this period.[2]

The bishops and the clergy in the United States were given the opportunity to observe the benefits derivable from sacred missions when in 1839 Pope Gregory XVI (1831-1846) sent Charles Forbin-Janson (1785-1844), the Bishop of Nancy and Toul, France, on a missionary tour through the United States and Canada. For two

[1] E.g., Council of Cashel (1863)—*Coll. Lac.*, III, 829; Council of Prague (1860)—*op. cit.*, V, 480; II Plenary Council of Baltimore (1866)—*op. cit.*, III, 525-526.

[2] E.g., Pius IX, ep. encycl. *Nostis et Nobiscum*, 8 dec. 1849—*Fontes*, n. 508; Meeting of the Bishops of Bavaria in Würzburg (1848)—*Coll. Lac.*, V, 981c.

years he gave missions to the people and retreats to the clergy with remarkable success. Pope Gregory XVI made Bishop Forbin-Janson a Roman Count and an Assistant at the Pontifical Throne in recognition of his service in demonstrating the benefits of sacred missions to the American people.[3]

B. The Quasi-religious

In some cases the missionary bands of secular priests which had been established in many dioceses formed into quasi-religious groups, but still called themselves secular priests. One of the most prominent of these was the *Congregation of the Most Precious Blood,* which was founded in 1814, in Giano near Rome, by Blessed Gaspare del Bufalo (1786-1837) at the request of Pope Pius VII (1800-1823). It was the intention of the Holy Father that the newly-founded society should give sacred missions throughout the Papal States, and as headquarters for this work he gave the Precious Blood Fathers the Convent of San Felice in Giano. Six other missions in the Roman States were established by 1820, and by the end of the nineteenth century the Congregation had spread into other countries of Europe and to America.[4]

In 1858, Isaac Hecker (1819-1888) and seven of his companions who had been Redemptorists obtained their release from that Congregation and founded a new group, the *Missionary Society of St. Paul,* for the giving of missions and for the conducting of other apostolic work. The Society began in Rome, but it soon transferred its activities to New York, where it was immediately approved by Archbishop Hughes (1850-1864). Although the conversion of America was their primary purpose, and non-Catholic missions the most prominent of their activities, the Paulists also became active in giving sacred missions for the faithful. The Paulists worked closely with the secular clergy in training diocesan missionary bands. An Apostolic Mission House was opened in 1903 on the grounds of the

[3] Maes, "Charles-Auguste-Marie-Joseph Comte de Forbin-Janson," *CE,* VI, 133-144.

[4] Mueller, "Congregation of the Most Precious Blood"—*CE,* XII, 373-374.

Catholic University in Washington, D. C., for the training of diocesan missionaries.[5]

C. The Religious Orders and Congregations

The Vincentians, Redemptorists, Jesuits, and others of the older religious Orders such as the Augustinians, the Franciscans, the Dominicans, and the Carmelites, contributed much to the development of sacred missions during the nineteenth century. There were founded also several new societies in which the giving of sacred missions was acknowledged as one of the principal activities.

The Society of the Priests of Mercy of the Immaculate Conception was founded in 1808 at Paris, France, for the purpose of doing mission work. The *Mercy Fathers* soon spread through many countries of the world, including America.[6]

The *Missionaries of Provence,* France, began their work in 1816. This Congregation was approved and received the title of *Oblates of Mary Immaculate* in a brief which Pope Leo XII (1823-1829) issued on February 17, 1826. The founder and first Superior General was Charles Joseph de Mazenod (1782-1861), who later became the Bishop of Marseilles (1837-1861). The purpose of the Congregation was to revive the spirit of faith among rural and industrial populations by means of missions and retreats. They became very successful in this work and in the foreign missions.[7]

In 1817, at Lyons, France, the *Society of Mary* was founded by the Venerable Jean Claude-Marie Colin (1790-1875) and his companions. The purpose of the Society was to perform missionary work in the rural districts. Approval was given by Pope Gregory XVI on April 29, 1836. The *Marist Fathers* became engaged in the

[5] Doyle, "The Apostolic Missionary House," *The Catholic Church in the United States of America* (3 vols., New York: The Catholic Editing Co., 1912-1914), I, 459-467.

[6] Bishop Forbin-Janson and Abbé Jean Baptiste Rauzan (1757-1847) collaborated in founding this society. Pope Gregory XVI gave his approval on February 18, 1834, in the bull *Ad supremum—Bull. Rom. Cont.,* XIX, 308-312.

[7] Cf. Ortolan, *Les Oblats de Marie Immaculée* (2 vols., Paris, 1915).

foreign missions of Oceania, but also took an active part in the development of parochial missions in Europe and America.[8]

The *Brothers of St. Joseph,* founded in 1820, and the *Auxiliary Priests of Mans,* France, founded in 1835, were combined into the *Congregation of the Holy Cross* in 1837 largely through the efforts of Basile-Antoine Moreau (1799-1870). The *Holy Cross Fathers* devoted themselves both to the foreign missions and to parochial mission work in various parts of the world.[9]

ARTICLE 2. LEGISLATION ON SACRED MISSIONS

A. The Holy See

Pope Gregory XVI, in 1834, extended to all who gave sacred missions, irrespective of the religious communities to which the missionaries belonged, the privilege of granting a plenary indulgence to those who attended the missions. The Pontiff also granted a plenary indulgence for the benefit of the sick who could not attend the sacred missions, provided that they had at home complied with the required conditions.[10]

The development of sacred missions received further encouragement from Pope Pius IX (1846-1878). Aware of the dangerous errors which were prevalent during the nineteenth century, the Pope called upon bishops and pastors to be mindful of providing proper instruction for their people. He urged them to preach by word and example.[11] The Holy Father recommended that suitable priests be specially trained for the giving of sacred missions to the people. These missions, the Pontiff pointed out, would not only cause sinners to do penance, but would also strengthen the faithful and help their spiritual progress.[12] Missionaries were urged to prepare carefully by reading, prayer, and meditation, and then give the fruit of their labors to the people in the form of these missions.[13]

[8] *Constitutiones Presbyterorum Societatis Mariae* (Augustae Taurinorum: Schola Typographica Salesiana, 1923), pp. 140-151, 242-262.

[9] Cavanaugh, *The Priests of the Holy Cross* (Notre Dame, Ind., 1905).

[10] *Bull. Rom. Cont.*, XIX. 449.

[11] Ep. encycl. *Qui pluribus,* 9 nov. 1846—*Fontes,* n. 504.

[12] Ep. encycl. *Nostis et Nobiscum,* 8 dec. 1849—*op. cit.,* n. 508.

[13] Ep. encycl. *Singulari quidem,* 17 mart. 1856—*op. cit.,* n. 521.

The Sacred Congregation for the Propagation of the Faith, in 1869, issued to the Vicars Apostolic of the East Indies an Instruction which called attention to the value of sacred missions for those under their care, and urged them to introduce missions into their vicariates.[14]

There was no specific mention of sacred missions in the abbreviated Vatican Council of 1869-1870, but certain recommendations were made in a proposal presented to the Council by the bishops of the Province of Naples. They asked for the enactment of a law requiring that a band of priests be specially trained and appointed to give sacred missions in every diocese.[15]

The Letter *Testem benevolentiae* of Pope Leo XIII (1878-1903), directed to America in 1899, approved both missions for Catholics and for non-Catholics as an excellent method of instruction in the Catholic religion.[16]

B. Local Ecclesiastical Legislation

The local ecclesiastical legislation concerning sacred missions in the nineteenth century may well be summarized by the following table which indicates chronologically the councils and synods which dealth with sacred missions. The title of council will always mean a provincial council unless indicated otherwise. By the term meeting is to be understood a convocation of all of the bishops in a particular country although not having the form nor authority of a plenary council.

[14] S.C. de Prop. Fide, instr. (ad Vic. Cap. Indiar. Orient.), 8 sept. 1869, n. 33—*Fontes,* n. 4876.

[15] *Postulata Episcoporum Neapolitanorum,* Cap. III, xxviii.—*Coll. Lac.,* VII, 810a.

[16] Ep. *Testem benevolentiae,* 22 ian. 1899—*Acta Sanctae Sedis* (41 vols., Romae, 1865-1908), XXXI (1899), 478-479 (hereafter cited *ASS*); *Fontes,* n. 640.

Year	Title	Place	Force	Frequency	Those Urged or Obliged	Source
1822	Synod (National)	Hungary	urged	....	....	*Coll. Lac.*, V, 938d.
1844	Synod	Pondicherry	urged	....	....	*Op. cit.*, VI, 655.
1848	Meeting	Bavaria (Würzburg)	urged	....	....	*Op. cit.*, V, 981c.
1849	Council	Reims	urged	....	....	*Op. cit.*, IV, 131.
1849	Council	Tours	urged	....	....	*Op. cit.*, IV, 271
1850	Council	Albi	urged	....	those having care of souls	*Op. cit.*, IV, 430.
1850	Council	Bordeaux	urged	....	pastors	*Op. cit.*, IV, 502.
1850	Council	Aix	ordered	every 6 yrs. or at least every 10 yrs.	pastors	*Op. cit.*, IV, 1002-1020.
1850	Council	Lyons	urged	....	....	*Op. cit.*, IV, 281.
1850	Council	Bourges	ordered	every 7 yrs.	pastors	*Op. cit.*, IV, 1128d.
1850	Council	Toulouse	urged	discretion of bishop	bishops	*Op. cit.*, IV, 1059c.
1850	Council	Thurles	urged	....	....	*Op. cit.*, III, 767.
1850	Meeting	Bavaria (Freising)	urged	....	....	*Op. cit.*, V, 1172.
1850	Council	Sienna	urged	....	....	*Op. cit.*, VI, 261, 280.
1850	Council	Pisa	ordered	continually	....	*Op. cit.*, VI, 238, 251.
1850	Council	Loreto	ordered	every 10 yrs., renewal every 5 yrs.	....	*Op. cit.*, VI, 800-809.

Year	Title	Place	Force	Frequency	Those Urged or Obliged	Source
1850	Council	Sicily	urged	....	....	*Op. cit.*, VI, 818.
1851	Meeting	Upper Rhine (Freiburg)	urged	....	....	*Op. cit.*, V, 1211a.
1851	Council	Auch	urged	....	....	*Op. cit.*, IV, 1203.
1852	Council	Westminster	urged	as often as expedient	bishops	*Op. cit.*, III, 1354.
1853	Council	Reims	urged	....	....	*Op. cit.*, IV, 174.
1853	Council	Cashel	ordered	....	bishops	*Op. cit.*, III, 829.
1853	Council	Dublin	urged	....	bishops	*Op. cit.*, III, 811.
1854	Council	Tuam	urged	....	bishops	*Op. cit.*, III, 862.
1855	Council	Ravenna	ordered	every 3 or 4 yrs.	pastors	*Op. cit.*, VI, 187, 195.
1856	Council	Austria	urged	....	....	*Op. cit.*, V, 1246.
1858	Council	Vienna	urged for all and ordered for large parishes	....	pastors	*Op. cit.*, V, 186b, c.
1858	Council	Strigonia	ordered	....	bishops	*Op. cit.*, V, 762.
1858	Council [17]	Cincinnati	urged	....	....	*Op. cit.*, III, 210.
1859	Council	Urbino	ordered	at least every 10 yrs. and every 5 yrs. in cities	bishops	*Op. cit.*, VI, 69-70.
1859	Council	Westminster	urged	....	....	*Op. cit.*, III, 1354b.

17 The council urged also that some permanent method of holding sacred missions be adapted in each diocese of the province.

Year	*Title*	*Place*	*Force*	*Frequency*	*Those Urged or Obliged*	*Source*
1860	Council	Prague	ordered	....	pastors	*Op. cit.*, V, 480b.
1863	Council	Calocza	urged	....	....	*Op. cit.*, V, 713.
1860	Council	Cologne	urged	....	....	*Op. cit.*, V, 371.
1865	Council [18]	Quebec	urged	....	....	*Op. cit.*, III, 674a, b.
1865	Council	Utrecht	urged	....	pastors	*Op. cit.*, V, 882b.
1866	Council [19] (Plenary)	Baltimore	urged	....	bishops	*Op. cit.*, III, 525-526.
1867	Synod	Paderborn	ordered	....	pastors	20
1867	Council	Port of Spain	urged	....	....	*Coll. Lac.*, III, 1114d.
1868	Council	New Granada	ordered	....	....	*Op. cit.*, VI, 539-544.
1868	Synod	Boston	ordered	every 3 or 4 yrs.	pastors	*Constitutiones Dioecesanae II Synodi Dioecesis Bostoniensis, anno 1868* (Boston, 1868), n. 216.
1869	Council	Baltimore	ordered	....	pastors	*Coll. Lac.*, III, 588d.
1869	Council	Quito	ordered	....	....	*Op. cit.*, VI, 436.
1869	Synod	Smyrna	urged	....	....	*Op. cit.*, VI, 573d.

[18] Bishops were urged by this council to select and train both secular and religious clergy for the task of giving sacred missions.

[19] Bishops were urged by this council to form mission bands in each diocese. Missionaries had to be approved by the ordinary before they conducted missions in a diocese.

[20] *Archiv fur katholisches Kirchenrecht* (Innsbruck, 1859-1861; Mainz 1862—), XV (1867), 99 (hereafter cited *AKKR*).

Year	*Title*	*Place*	*Force*	*Frequency*	*Those Urged or Obliged*	*Source*
1875	Council (Plenary)	Maynooth	urged	....	bishops	*Acta et Decreta Synodi Plenariae Episcoporum Hiberniae apud Maynutiam, anno 1875* (Dublin, 1877), nn. 19-20.
1884	Synod	Albany	ordered	every 3 or 4 yrs.	pastors	*Synodus Dioecesis Albanensis Tertia, anno 1884* (Albany, 1884), n. 27.
1886	Synod	Buffalo	ordered	every 3 or 4 yrs.	pastors	*Synodus Dioecesis Buffalensis Vigesima, anno 1884* (Buffalo, 1884), Tit. XIV.
1886	Synod	Ogdensburg	ordered	every 3 or 4 yrs.	pastors	*Synodus Dioecesana II Ogdensburgensis, anno 1886* (Ogdensburg, 1886), n. 46.
1886	Synod	Manchester	ordered	every 4 or 5 yrs.	pastors	*Synodus Dioecesana Prima Manchesteriensis, anno 1886* (Manchester, 1886), n. 31.
1886	Synod	Richmond	ordered	every 5 yrs.	pastors	*Acta et Statuta Synodi Richmondiensis Secundae, anno 1886* (Richmond, 1886), n. 106.

Year	Title	Place	Force	Frequency	Those Urged or Obliged	Source
1886	Synod	New York	ordered	every 3 or 4 yrs.	pastors	*Synodus Dioecesana Neo-Eboracensis Quinta, anno 1886* (New York, 1886), n. 42.
1887	Synod	Syracuse	ordered	every 3 or 4 yrs.	pastors	*Dioecesana Prima Syracusensis Synodus, anno 1887* (Syracuse, 1887), n. 42.
1894	Synod	Brooklyn	ordered	every 3 or 4 yrs.	pastors	*Constitutiones Dioecesanae Brooklyniensis Tertiae Synodi, anno 1894* (Brooklyn, 1894), n. 45.
1895	Council [21] (Plenary)	Australia	ordered	every 3 or 5 yrs.	bishops and pastors	*Acta et Decreta Concilii Plenarii Australiensis II, anno 1895* (Sydney, 1898), decr. 263, 267, 269.
1897	Synod	Trenton	ordered	every 5 yrs.	pastors	*Synodus Trentonensis II, anno 1897* (Trenton, 1897), n. 216.

21 Missionaries were warned by this council not to interfere in the internal affairs of the parish nor to start up new confraternities without the permission of the bishop and the pastor. Their stipend was fixed at five pounds sterling for every week.

Year	Title	Place	Force	Frequency	Those Urged or Obliged	Source
1899	Council [22]	Latin America	ordered	....	bishops	*Acta et Decreta Concilii Plenarii Americae Latinae, anno 1899* (Romae, 1902; appendix, Romae, 1906), decr. 69.

22 The council ordered that every mission should include a sermon on hell.

From this representative, although far from exhaustive, list of councils and synods which enacted legislation on sacred missions during the nineteenth century, the growing obligation can be easily traced. It is to be noted that the obligation seemed to rest both on the bishops and on the pastors to see that sacred missions were held. The recommendation of St. Alphonsus that pastors should have a mission every four or five years was followed very closely, and in some cases adopted *verbatim* in the legislation.[23]

C. Secular Law

The reaction of civil governments toward sacred missions during the nineteenth century was mixed and changeable. After the terror of the French Revolution had subsided and Napoleon I had taken control in France, missions were first approved by the dictator and even sponsored by him in some parts of France. In September, 1809, however, sacred missions were prohibited in France by order of Napoleon, who was furious because the Church would not submit to his plans.[24]

In Austria, sacred missions progressed during the reign of Maria Theresa (1740-80) in the eighteenth century, and then were prohibited by her successor, Joseph II (1780-1790), who had been co-regent with his mother (1765-1780). Leopold II (1790-1792) was not opposed to sacred missions, but his successor, Francis I (1792-1835), although ostensibly a good Catholic, was devoted to the memory of his uncle, Joseph II, and followed his example in his interference with sacred missions. A concordat was arranged, under Francis Joseph I (1848-1916), which gave comparative freedom to the work of sacred missions.

Neighboring Germany, however, was not so fortunate, for the Church had to contend with the *Kulturkampf*, precipitated by Bismarck (1815-1898). In 1872 the Jesuits were expelled, and in the following year the Redemptorists, the Vincentians, and the Holy Ghost Fathers were also driven out of Germany. Since these reli-

[23] E.g., the Council of Ravenna (1865)—*Coll. Lac.*, VI, 187, 195; cf. St. Alphonsus Liguori, *Homo Apostolicus*, Tract. VII, n. 31, p. 144.

[24] *Wernz, Ius Decretalium,* III, 50.

gious had been doing the major part of the work in sacred missions, their expulsion was a serious handicap. The so-called *Kanzelpanagraf* or pulpit law (1871) and the infamous *May* laws (1873) were especially aggravating to the cause of sacred missions. Although the *Kulturkampf* was relaxed toward the close of the nineteenth century, the laws against sacred missions remained on the statute books a long time afterwards.[25]

[25] Hinschius, *System des katholischen Kirchenrechts,* IV, 489; Kassiepe, *Die katholische Volksmission in der neuen Zeit, Grandsätzliches und Praktisches für Seelsorger* (Paderborn: Verlag Ferdinand Schöningh, 1934), pp. 12-13.

CHAPTER V

THE TWENTIETH CENTURY

ARTICLE 1. THE OBLIGATION OF HOLDING SACRED MISSIONS AS COMMONLY UNDERSTOOD JUST BEFORE THE CODE

A. The Opinion of the Authors

MOST of the authors who wrote about sacred missions just before the Code were inclined to follow the standards set by St. Alphonsus Liguori. It was his opinion that a pastor could not in good faith refuse to provide the benefits of sacred missions for his people, and furthermore that a good pastor should have a mission every four or five years.[1] All admitted that there was not in the Church any universal law which obliged a pastor to hold sacred missions in his parish.

The general consensus was that, even if there were no particular legislation binding a pastor, yet it would be very imprudent for him not to hold sacred missions at least occasionally.[2] The belief that a pastor had a moral obligation to provide sacred missions for his flock at regular intervals found expression not only in canonical works, but in the writings of other ecclesiastical authors as well.[3]

[1] St. Alphonsus Liguori, *Homo Apostolicus,* Tract. VII, n. 31, p. 144.

[2] Wernz furnished the most detailed explanation of this opinion. Cf. *Ius Decretalium,* III, 52, note 59. Cf. also: Aertnys, *Theologia Pastoralis* (Paderborn, 1901), p. 31, nn. 257-260; Renninger, *Pastoral-Theologie* (Freiburg im Br., 1893), nn. 526-528.

[3] Schroeder, in his article "Missions, Catholic parochial" which was published in 1911, stated: "In the average American parish there is a mission every three years, in some every second year, and many make it an annual event."—*CE,* X, 394. Confer also the series of articles on parochial missions in *The American Ecclesiastical Review* (Philadelphia, 1889-1943; Washington, D. C., 1944—; and published as *The Ecclesiastical Review,* July, 1905-December, 1943), II (1890), 86, 92, 161, 173, 178, 191, 193, 194, 196, 208 (hereafter cited *AER* and *ER* respectively).

The right of the bishop to send missionaries into a parish, regardless of whether it was a religious or a secular parish, if he thought that it was necessary for ensuring the instruction of the faithful, was pointed out by some authors.[4]

B. The Practice of the Bishops

There seems to be no indication that, in the years just before the Code, any of the bishops were opposed to sacred missions. Some, naturally, were more in favor of them than others. The various councils and synods which were held throughout the nineteenth century indicated that most bishops were conscious of the need and utility of sacred missions, even though they may not have provided a specific obligation.[5]

C. The Practice of the Pastors

The obligation of holding sacred missions was, in the years just before the Code, interpreted variously in the practice of the pastors. The intervals between the missions ranged respectively from one to ten years. The majority of the pastors seemed conscious of an obligation to provide some kind of extraordinary spiritual exercises, but the opinions on the exact types and methods, and regarding the best time for such exercises or missions, were widely divergent. There was some criticism of the spectacular methods used by some missionaries, and there were occasional complaints about their interference in the internal affairs of parishes. The general practice for the average pastor of a heavily populated district, regardless of the country, was to have a mission at least every five or six years. The interval between missions for the average pastor in a rural district was about nine or ten years.[6] This custom did not obtain in missionary countries such as China or India, for the sacred missions were practically identified with the general instruction work in the foreign missions.

[4] E.g., Wernz, *Ius Decretalium,* III, 53.

[5] Couly, "Des missions"—*Le Canoniste,* XLVI (1924), 290.

[6] Cf. series of articles in *AER,* XI (1894), 81, 86, 102, 161, 173, 196, 208, 219.

Article 2. Legislation on Sacred Missions

A. The Holy See

In 1903 Pope Leo XIII addressed to the Church in the Philippine Islands a letter in which he strongly recommended the work of sacred missions and urged that they be given regularly.[7] Alarmed at the expulsion of religious from France by the anti-clerical government, and at the consequent effect it would have on sacred missions, Pope Pius X (1903-1914), in a letter to a meeting of the French hierarchy, strongly urged that diocesan missionaries be trained for this important work.[8] The Pontiff admitted that his recommendation was a difficult one to follow in view of the scarcity of the priests, but he urged them to do what they could under the circumstances. Furthermore, Pope Pius X stated that by favoring sacred missions he did not mean to exclude other laudable and pious exercises.

On March 19, 1904, Pope Pius X issued his famous *motu proprio, Arduum sane munus,* in which he called for a codification of the laws of the universal Church, and for this purpose he set up a Pontifical Commission made up of Cardinals.[9] Finally the *Codex Iuris Canonici* was promulgated by Pope Benedict XV (1914-1922) by means of the Constitution *Providentissima* of May 27, 1917, which decreed that the Code would begin to have the force of law from the feast of Pentecost of the following year, or May 19, 1918.[10]

The obligation of holding sacred missions in parishes was definitely fixed in canon 1349 of the Code of Canon Law, which placed on ordinaries the obligation to see that pastors have what is called a sacred mission at least every ten years. The second part of the canon declared that this obligation related to religious pastors as well. Since the enactment of the Code the only pronouncement on sacred missions published as yet (1949) by the Holy See was the apostolic letter of Pope Pius XI (1922-1939), in which on March 17, 1923, he proclaimed St. Leonard of Port Maurice to be the patron of missions among Catholics.[11]

[7] *Analecta Ecclesiastica* (18 vols., Romae, 1893-1911), X (1903), 6.
[8] *AAS,* III (1911), 268-269.
[9] *ASS,* XXXVI (1904), 549.
[10] *AAS,* pars II (1917).
[11] *AAS,* XV (1923), 196.

B. Local Ecclesiastical Legislation

In the twentieth century before the Code, legislation on sacred missions, by particular councils and synods, corresponded closely to that of the nineteenth century. The promulgation of the Code did not make much difference as far as sacred missions were concerned. Most dioceses were already holding sacred missions regularly. Many Councils and synods were content to repeat the words of the Code concerning sacred missions. In many more dioceses, however, the obligation of holding sacred missions was made even more specific and exacting.

For the most part the particular legislation is directed at pastors but the obligation of bishops to enforce the law contained in canon 1349 is always to be understood. The particular legislation is well illustrated by the table on the following pages.

Year	Title	Place	Force	Frequency	Those Urged or Obliged	Source
1903	Synod	Grand Rapids	urged	....	pastors	*Synodus Grandormensis I, anno 1903* (Grand Rapids, 1903), n. 266.
1909	Synod	Little Rock	ordered	every 3 or 5 yrs.	pastors	*Synodus Dioecesana Petriculana Prima, anno 1909* (Little Rock, 1909), n. 20.
1914	Synod	Rochester	ordered	every 5 yrs.	pastors	*Synodus Roffensis Tertia, anno 1914* (Rochester, 1914), n. 67.
1916	Synod	Rockford	ordered	every 3 yrs.	pastors	*Synodus Dioecesana Rockfordensis Prima, anno 1916* (Mayer et Miller: Chicageni, 1916), n. 37.
1917	Synod	Puerto Rico	urged	....	pastors	*Sinodo Diocesano del Obispado de Puerto Rico, 1917* (Puerto Rico, 1917), n. 282.
1919	Synod	Boston	ordered	every 3 or 4 yrs.	pastors	*Constitutiones Dioecesanae Synodi Bostoniensis Sextae, anno 1919* (Boston, 1919), n. 152.
1920	Synod	Cincinnati	ordered	repeats Code	pastors	*Synodus Dioecesana Cincinnatensis Quarta, anno 1920* (Cincinnati, 1920), n. 32.

Year	Title	Place	Force	Frequency	Those Urged or Obliged	Source
1920	Synod	Pittsburgh	ordered	every 5 yrs.	pastors	*Statuta Dioecesis Pittsburgensis IV Synodi, anno 1920* (Pittsburgh, 1920), n. 209.
1920	Synod	Green Bay	ordered	every 5 yrs.	pastors	*Constitutiones Dioeceseos Sinus Viridis Quartae Synodi Dioecesanae, anno 1920* (Pulaski, Mich.: Typis Franciscanae Typographiae, 1921), n. 63.
1920	Council (Plenary)	Sicily	ordered	repeats Code	pastors	*Concilium Plenarium Siculum, Panormi anno habitum* (Romae: Typ. polygl. Vaticanis, 1921), can. 26 (cited by McVann on p. 151).
1920	Council	Malines	ordered	every 7 yrs. and lasting from 8 to 10 days	pastors	*Acta et Decreta Concilii Provincialis Mechliniensis IV, anno 1920* (Mechliniae: H. Dessain, 1923), n. 211.
1921	Synod	Syracuse	ordered	every 3 yrs. or at least every 10 yrs.	pastors	*Synodus Dioecesana Syracusiensis Undecima, anno 1921* (Syracuse, 1921), n. 38.

Year	*Title*	*Place*	*Force*	*Frequency*	*Those Urged or Obliged*	*Source*
1921	Synod	Crookston	ordered	repeats Code	pastors	*First Diocesan Synod of Crookston, 1921* (St. Louis: Herder, 1923), n. 396.
1921	Synod	Mobile	ordered	repeats Code	pastors	*Decreta Synodi Dioecesanae Mobiliensis Tertiae, anno 1921* (Mobile, 1921), n. 75.
1922	Synod	Altoona	ordered	repeats Code	pastors	*I Synodus Altunensis, anno 1922* (Altoona, 1922), n. 85.
1922	Synod	Leavenworth	ordered	repeats Code	pastors	*Statuta Dioecesanae Synodi Quartae Leavenworthensis, anno 1922* (Leavenworth, 1922), n. 195.
1922	Synod	New Orleans	ordered	every 5 yrs.	pastors	*Synodus Novae Aureliae Sexta, anno 1922* (New Orleans, 1922), n. 261.
1922	Synod	Natchez	ordered	every 5 yrs.	pastors	*Constitutiones Dioecesis Natchensis, anno 1922* (Natchez, 1922), n. 261.
1923	Synod	Alexandria	ordered	every 5 yrs.	pastors	*Dioecesana Synodus Alexandriae, anno 1923* (Alexandria, La., 1923), n. 14.

Year	Title	Place	Force	Frequency	Those Urged or Obliged	Source
1923	Synod	Des Moines	ordered	every 5 yrs.	pastors	*Code of the Diocese of Des Moines Decreed in Diocesan Synod on June 15, 1923* (Des Moines, 1923), n. 281.
1923	Synod	Wheeling	ordered	repeats Code	pastors	*Statutes of the Diocese of Wheeling Promulgated at the Diocesan Synod, 1923* (Wheeling, 1923), n. 338.
1923	Synod [12]	Strasbourg	ordered	repeats Code	pastors	*Statuta Synodalia Dioecesis Argentinensis, anno 1923* (Argentorati Typis Francisci Xaverii Le Roux, 1923), nn. 542-547.
1924	Council	Seville	ordered	repeats Code	pastors	*Concilium Provinciale Hispalense, anno 1924* (Romae: typ. polygl. Vaticanis, 1926; cited by McVann on p. 151), can. 260.

[12] This synod made the obligation more specific by ordering that the missions which were held in cities and suburbs should be general missions.

Year	Title	Place	Place	Frequency	Those Urged or Obliged	Source
1924	Council [18]	China	allowed	discretion of ordinary	quasi-pastors	*Primum Concilium Sinense, anno 1924* (Zi-Ka-Wei: Typographia Missionis Catholicae, 1929), n. 116.
1924	Synod	Buffalo	ordered	every 5 yrs.	pastors	*Synodus Dioecesana Buffalensis Vigesima Septima, anno 1924* (Buffalo, 1924), art. 449.
1925	Synod	Charleston	ordered	every 3 yrs.	pastors	*Constitutiones Dioecesanae Synodi Septimae Decimae Carolpolitanae, anno 1925* (Charleston, 1925), n. 190.
1926	Council (Plenary)	Portugal	ordered	repeats Code	bishops and pastors	*Concilium Plenarium Lusitanum, anno 1926* (cited by McVann on p, 152), can. 413.

[18] Missions could be held for the faithful in China if certain precautions were taken. The precautions were:

1. *De tempore.* Nonnisi extra consuetum missionis tempus huiusmodi exercitia tradantur, et quando populus operibus in campis vel in agris incumbere non cogatur.

2. *De convocandis.* Praesertim convocentur coadiutores missionarii in quibus catechistae, priores et notabiles, etc. . . . separatim a mulieribus viri exerceantur.

3. *De praedicatore.* Si exercitia proprius missionarius ipse tradit, optandum est ut, praesertim in confessionibus excipiendis, ab uno alterove sacerdote adiuvetur.

Year	Title	Place	Force	Frequency	Those Urged or Obliged	Source
1926	Synod	Brooklyn	ordered	every 5 yrs.	pastors	*Synodus Dioecesana Brooklyniensis Quinta, anno 1926* (Brooklyn, 1926), n. 45.
1927	Synod	Fort Wayne	ordered	repeats Code	pastors	*Synodus Dioecesana Prima Wayne Castrensis, anno 1927* (Fort Wayne, 1927), can. 31.
1927	Council (Plenary)	Piedmont	ordered	every 5 yrs.	bishops and pastors	*Acta Concilii Plenarii Pedemontani, Taurini, anno 1927* (Taurini: Marietti, 1928; McVann, p. 151), can. 14.
1927	Council (Plenary)	Maynooth	ordered	every 5 yrs.	bishops and pastors	*Acta et Decreta Concilii Plenarii Episcoporum Hiberniae apud Maynutiam, anno 1927* (Dublin: Brown et Nolan, 1929), decr. 375.
1927	Synod	Los Angeles	ordered and exhorted	every 10 yrs. every 5 yrs.	pastors	*Statuta Dioecesana Angelorum et Sancti Didaci Lata ac Promulgata in Synodo Quinta, anno 1927* (St. Louis: Herder, 1927), n. 184.

Year	*Title*	*Place*	*Force*	*Frequency*	*Those Urged or Obliged*	*Source*
1927	Synod	Dallas	ordered	every 5 yrs.	pastors	*Synodus Dioecesana Dallasensis Secunda, anno 1927* (Dallas, 1927), nn. 50, 195.
1927	Synod	Ogdensburg	ordered	every 5 yrs.	pastors	*Statuta Dioecesis Ogdensburgensis XIII Synodi, anno 1928* (Ogdensburg, 1928), n. 54.
1928	Council	Venice	ordered	repeats Code	bishops and pastors	*Concilii Venetii Provincialis II: Acta et Decreta, anno 1928* (Venetis; cited by McVann on p. 152), decr. 440.
1929	Synod	Monterey-Fresno	ordered	repeats Code	pastors	*Montereyensis - Fresnensis Synodus Prima, anno 1929* (Monterey-Fresno, 1929), n. 93.
1929	Synod	St. Louis	ordered	every 5 yrs.	pastors	*Dioecesana Synodus Sancti Ludovici Septima, anno 1929* (St. Louis, 1929), n. 146.
1929	Synod	Salt Lake City	ordered	every 5 yrs. or at least every 10 yrs.	pastors	*Statuta Dioecesis Lacus Salsi Lata ac Promulgata in Synodo Dioecesana Prima, anno 1929* (Salt Lake City, 1929), n. 183.

Year	*Title*	*Force*	*Force*	*Frequency*	*Those Urged or Obliged*	*Source*
1930	Synod	El Paso	ordered	every 3 yrs.	pastors	*Synodus Dioecesana Elpasensis Prima, anno 1930* (El Paso, 1930), n. 132.
1930	Council	Valladolid	ordered	repeats Code	bishops and pastors	*Concilium II Provinciale Vallisoletanum, anno 1930* (Romae, typ. polygl. Vaticanis, 1932; cited by McVann on p. 152), decr. 272.
1930	Council	Toledo (Spain)	ordered	every 5 yrs.	bishops and pastors	*Decreta Concilii Provincialis Toletanae, anno 1930* (Toletani: typ. editor. Catholicae Toletanae, 1933; cited by McVann on p. 152), decr. 313.
1932	Council (Plenary)	North Cen. Italy	ordered	repeats Code	bishops and pastors	*Concilium Plenarium Aemilianae et Flaminiae Regionis, Bononiae anno 1932 habitum* (Parmae: ex typ. Fresching, 1933; cited by McVann on p. 152), decr. 32.
1932	Synod	Davenport	ordered	every 5 yrs.	pastors	*The Third Synod of Davenport, 1932* (Davenport, 1932), n. 53.

Year	*Title*	*Place*	*Force*	*Frequency*	*Those Urged or Obliged*	*Source*
1932	Council	Portland in Oregon	ordered	every 3 yrs.	bishops and pastors	*Acta et Decreta Concilii Portlandensis in Oregon IV, anno 1932* (Portland, 1934), decr. 38.
1933	Council	Tuam	ordered	repeats Code	bishops and pastors	*Acta et Decreta Concilii Provincialis Tuamensis, anno 1933* (Galviae: O'Gorman, 1935), n. 30.
1933	Synod	Richmond	ordered	every 5 yrs.	pastors	*Synodus Dioecesana Richmondiensis Tertia, anno 1933* (Richmond, 1933), n. 178.
1934	Synod	Lincoln	ordered and urged	every 10 yrs. every 5 yrs.	pastors	*Statutes of the Diocese of Lincoln, First Synod 1934* (Lincoln, 1934), n. 5.
1934	Synod	Omaha	ordered	every 5 yrs.	pastors	*Synodus Dioecesana Omahensis, anno 1934* (Omaha, 1934), n. 338.
1934	Synod	Cajetan	ordered	repeats Code	pastors	*Synodus Dioecesana Cajetana Sexta, anno 1934* (M. D'Auria S. Sedes Apostolicae Typographis: Neapoli, 1935), constit. 25.
1935	Synod	Rochester	ordered	every 5 yrs.	pastors	*Synodius Roffensis Quinta, anno 1935* (Rochester, 1935), n. 37.

Year	Title	Place	Force	Frequency	Those Urged or Obliged	Source
1935	Synod	Great Falls	ordered	every 3 yrs. follows IV Prov. Con. Portland, Ore.	pastors	*Synodus Dioecesana Greatormensis Prima, anno 1935* (Great Falls, 1935), n. 30.
1935	Synod	Portland, Ore.	ordered	every 3 yrs. follows IV Prov. Con. Portland, Ore.	pastors	*Synodus Archidioesana Portlandensis in Oregon, anno 1935* (Portland, Ore., 1935), n. 30.
1936	Synod	Trenton	ordered	every 5 yrs.	pastors	*Synodus Dioecesana Trentonensis Tertia, anno 1936* (Trenton, 1936), n. 266.
1936	Synod	San Francisco	ordered	every 2 yrs.	pastors	*Statuta Archidioecesanae Synodi Secundae Sancti Francisci, anno 1936* (San Francisco, 1936), n. 343.
1936	Synod	San Cristobal	ordered	repeats Code	pastors	*Estatutos Sinodales de la Diocesis de San Cristobal, Venezuela, 1936* (San Cristobal: Typographia Diocesana, 1936), stat. 648-650.
1938	Synod	Seattle	ordered	every 3 yrs. follows IV Prov. Con. Portland, Ore.	pastors	*Synodus Dioecesana Seattlensis Quinta, anno 1938* (Seattle: Typis Metropolitanis, 1938), n. 81.

Year	Title	Place	Force	Frequency	Those Urged or Obliged	Source
1939	Synod	Belleville	ordered	every 5 yrs.	pastors	*Statuta Dioecesis Bellevillensis, V Synodus, anno 1939* (Belleville, 1939), n. 186.
1939	Synod	Spokane	ordered	every 3 yrs. follows IV Prov. Con. Portland, Ore.	pastors	*Statuta Dioecesanae Synodi Spokanensis Primae, anno 1939* (Spokane, 1939), n. 154.
1939	Synod	Savannah-Atlanta	ordered	every 3 yrs.	pastors	*Statuta Dioecesis Savannensis-Atlantensis, I Synodus, anno 1939* (Atlanta, 1939), n. 132.
1940	Synod	Quebec	ordered	every 5 yrs.	pastors	*Acta et Decreta Synodi Dioecesanae Quebecensis Secundae, anno 1940* (Quebeci, 1940), decr. 403.
1941	Synod	Boise	ordered	every 3 yrs. follows IV Prov. Con. Portland, Ore.	pastors	*Synodus Dioecesana Xylopolitanae Secundae, anno 1941* (Boise, 1941), n. 3.
1941	Synod	Fargo	ordered	every 3 yrs.	pastors	*Synodus Dioecesis Fargensis Prima, anno 1941* (Milwaukee: Bruce, 1941), n. 527.

Year	*Title*	*Place*	*Force*	*Frequency*	*Those Urged or Obliged*	*Source*
1943	Synod	Owensboro	ordered	every 5 yrs.	pastors	*First Synod of the Diocese of Owensboro, The, 1943* (Owensboro, 1943), stat. 98.
1943	Synod	Toledo (Ohio)	ordered	every 5 yrs.	pastors	*Acta et Decreta Synodi Primae Toletanae in America, anno 1943* (Toledo, Ohio, 1943), n. 291.
1943	Synod	Lafayette (La.)	ordered	every 5 yrs.	pastors	*Constitutions of the Diocese of Lafayette, 1943* (Lafayette, La., 1943), n. 283.
1943	Synod	Harrisburg	ordered	every 3 yrs.	pastors	*Ninth Synod of Harrisburg, The, 1943* (Harrisburg, 1943), n. 63.
1947	Synod	Indianapolis	ordered	every 5 yrs.	pastors	*Synodus Archidioeceseos Indianapolitanae (I) Septima, anno 1947* (Indianapolis, 1947), n. 115.
1948	Synod	Pueblo	ordered	every 5 yrs.	pastors	*Statutes of the Diocese of Pueblo, First Diocesan Synod, 1948* (Pueblo, 1948), stat. 256.

In retrospect, it may be noted that the average maximum interval upon which the holding of a parish mission is to be repeated is five years. For the thirty years which have passed since the advent of the Code, this rule was found applicable not only in the United States, but in other countries as well.

C. Secular Law

The holding of sacred missions in France was under severe inhibition at the beginning of the twentieth century. That followed naturally upon the anti-clerical government's expulsion of the religious Orders from the country. Specific laws against missions were also passed in France at that time. Gradually these laws were discarded, the religious Orders were permitted to return, and after the First World War there was very little interference with the work of holding missions.[14]

The persecution of religion in Russia and in Mexico, and the interference with religion in Germany and in other countries, naturally either destroyed or hampered the work of sacred missions, but no specific laws were directed against them as such.

[14] Wernz, *Ius Decretalium,* III, 50 (Wernz also discussed at length when a civil government could lawfully prohibit the holding of sacred missions); Couly, "Des missions,"—*Le Canoniste,* XLVI (1924), 290.

Part II

Canonical Commentary

CHAPTER VI

THE OBLIGATION OF HOLDING SACRED MISSIONS AS STATED IN THE CODE

Article 1. Source of the Obligation

A. Authority of the Church

In the appraisal of an obligation of any kind it is often helpful to look first at the source of that obligation in order to determine what force it may have. The source of an ecclesiastical obligation lies in the authority of the Church to make laws. It may prove advantageous to point out briefly some of the fundamental concepts of the public law of the Church before one adverts to the particular obligation treated in this dissertation.

Man does not choose whether or not he wishes to belong to society. His birth into the world marks also his admission into society. A society may be defined as the union of a number of men for the purpose of obtaining the same end by the use of common means.[1] There must be some authority in every society in order that it may achieve its purpose. Authority is the right of obliging the members of a society to do the things that are necessary for obtaining the proper end of the society.[2]

A society exists either sovereign or dependent. A sovereign society is a moral person which is *sui iuris,* or, in other words, it is one

[1] Ottaviani, *Compendium Iuris Publici Ecclesiastici* (Romae: Typis Polyglottis Vaticanis, 1936), p. 11.

[2] Ottaviani, *op. cit.,* p. 36.

which has its personality independently of the will of any human legislator.[3] The power which is exercised by the authority in society is divided into legislative, judicial, and executive. The Catholic Church is a sovereign society and therefore has the right to exercise its authority in any of these three ways. The authority of the Church, in the exercise of its social power, does not depend upon the will of its members but rather upon the Will of its Divine Founder, and the power is wielded in His Name by the duly constituted rulers of the Church.[4] It is an accepted general rule that a society can exact from its members all those things which are necessary or useful for its end. The Church, therefore, can demand from the faithful those things which are necessary or useful for promoting the sanctification of souls.

Since it is a sovereign society, the Church acts entirely within its rights when it enacts and enforces laws. As the Code states: *"Nativum et proprium Ecclesiae ius est, independens a qualibet humana auctoritate, coercendi delinquentes sibi subditos poenis tum spiritualibus tum etiam temporalibus."* [5]

B. Authority of the Code

The Code of Canon Law, which is the body of laws made by the lawful ecclesiastical authority for the government of the Church, derives its authority from Almighty God through the Pope, the Vicar of Christ on earth. The universal legal authority of the Code is manifested through the words of Pope Benedict XV in promulgating the Code: ". . . We promulgate and We decree and order that the present Code, just as it is drawn up, have in future the force of law for the universal Church . . ." [6]

Unconditional legal force is to be accorded to each and all the canons, for in their import they are entirely regulative. In their

[3] Ottaviani, *op. cit.*, p. 26.

[4] Ottaviani, *op. cit.*, p. 144.

[5] Can. 2214.

[6] Const. *Providentissima Mater Ecclesia*, 27 maii 1917, translation in Cicognani, *Canon Law* (translated by J. M. O'Hara and F. Brennan, 2. ed., Westminster, Md.: The Newman Book Shop, reprinted in 1947), p. 432.

structure there is nothing of the purely narrative. A Pontifical Commission of Cardinals was established by Pope Benedict XV for the official interpretation of the Code.[7] The Commission's interpretation becomes compulsory for its acceptance and obligatory for its recognition whether it restates, explains, extends or restricts any of the Church's laws.[8]

Canon 6 is extremely important for the interpretation of all the canons in the Code, and is of vital importance for the canons which pertain to this dissertation. According to this canon, the Code retains the discipline hitherto in force although it makes some opportune changes. Laws which stood in opposition to the Code, whether they were universal or particular, went out of existence with the promulgation of the Code, unless with reference to the particular laws some provision was made for their continuance. When the present law restates the earlier law either in whole or in part, then in the same measure it is to be interpreted in harmony with the earlier interpretation. When there is doubt whether some provision of the canons differs from the earlier law, then there is not to be any departure from the import of the earlier law. One of the important ways in determining the force of an obligation, as remains to be done in this dissertation, is to discover what was the force of the obligation, if any, in the earlier law.

Article 2. Nature of the Obligation

A. Obligation of the Bishops

Can. 1349, § 1, "Ordinarii advigilent ut, saltem decimo quoque anno, sacram, quam vocant, missionem ad gregem sibi commissum habendam parochi curent."

The obligation is placed upon the ordinaries to see that the pastors hold sacred missions for their parishes. Although canon 1349, § 1, does not state who are to be classified as ordinaries in the fulfillment of this obligation, it is evident from the context and from the earlier

7 Motu prop. *Cum iuris canonici*, 15 sept. 1917—*AAS*, IX (1918), 434.
8 Cicognani, *Canon Law*, p. 434.

law that only the local ordinaries are meant here. The local ordinaries are specifically mentioned in canon 1349, § 2, "Parochus, etiam religiosus, in his missionibus instituendis mandatis Ordinarii loci stare debet."

The whole tenor of the previous legislation regarding sacred missions indicates that the ordinaries referred to in canon 1349 are the local ordinaries. The local ordinaries were given full power to regulate the time for sacred missions to be held, to draw up schedules for the visiting bands of missionaries, to send their own appointees to a parish,[9] and to grant faculties for preaching and for the hearing of confessions.[10]

Throughout Title XX of the Third Book in the Code of Canon Law, the responsibility for preaching the word of God is placed upon the bishop. He has the duty of preaching the Catholic Faith for his diocese just as the Pope must do for the universal Church.[11] The bishop is to grant the faculty to preach, and he is to protect the orthodoxy of doctrine. In harmony with the pre-Code law and with other canons in the Code concerning preaching, the obligation of canon 1349 evidently pertains only to the local ordinaries.

Since the holding of sacred missions is a matter which has for its end the spiritual welfare of the parishioners, the obligation of seeing that such missions are given rests upon the local ordinary and the pastor. In matters which pertain to parochial discipline, pastors, even though they are exempt religious, are subject to the authority of the local ordinary.[12]

While major religious superiors of exempt religious surely should be interested in the welfare of the souls entrusted to the pastoral care of their subjects, there is nothing to indicate that they are bound by the obligation of seeing that sacred missions are held in the parishes which may, in any manner, be staffed by religious.[13] As one author says, "Even in the case of a pastor who is an exempt

[9] S.C. Ep. et Reg., *Macerten.*, 7 mart. 1579—*Fontes,* n. 1353; S.C. Ep. et Reg., *Senen.*, 23 iul. 1694—*op. cit.*, n. 1816.

[10] Sess. V, *de ref.*, c. 2; XXIV, *de ref.*, c. 4.

[11] Can. 1327.

[12] Cann. 336; 343; 344; 631; 1336.

[13] McVann, p. 150.

religious, if the religious ordinary should insist that these missions be held, he will not be acting on the strength of this present canon, but rather as a religious superior who has dominative power over his subjects." [14] Religious are completely under the jurisdiction of the local ordinary with reference to sacred missions.[15] Major religious superiors of exempt religious are not to be included as ordinaries in canon 1349 despite the contention of Blat.[16]

Local ordinaries in this case include residential bishops, abbots or prelates *nullius,* diocesan administrators, and apostolic administrators. Vicars general are not included unless the bishops are impeded from acting. The obligation rests upon vicars and prefects apostolic as well, since no express exemption is indicated in canon 1349. In the case of missionary territories, however, where there are relatively small numbers of the faithful and few priests, the Holy See often leaves the holding of sacred missions to the discretion of the local ordinaries.[17]

Sacred missions for the faithful are, if possible, to be held also in mission countries, but naturally there are many extenuating circumstances which could allow a relaxation of the strict letter of the law. Frequently such missions are coupled with instructions for any pagans who may be induced to attend, and thus the giving of missions is frequently subjected to the special regulations of the Holy See.[18]

The obligation is placed upon the local ordinaries to see that pastors hold sacred missions. The ordinaries are to watch, "*advigilent.*" This word is used commonly in the Code to express a super-

[14] Keene, *Religious Ordinaries and Canon 198,* The Catholic University of America Canon Law Studies, n. 135 (Washington, D. C.: The Catholic University of America Press, 1942), pp. 93-94.

[15] Bondini, *De Privilegio Exemptionis seu de Regularium Immunitate ab Ordinariorum Locorum Iurisdictione prout in Novo Iuris Canonici Codice Sancitur* (Romae, 1919), p. 131.

[16] *Commentarium Textus Codicis Iuris Canonici,* Vol. IV (Romae: ex Typographia Pontificia in Instituto Pii IX, 1927), 334.

[17] S.C. de Prop. Fide, instr. (ad Vic. Ap. Indiar. Orient.), 8 sept. 1869—*Fontes,* n. 33; *Primum Concilium Sinense, anno 1924,* n. 116.

[18] Can. 1350, § 2.

visory obligation.[19] In general, the force of the word signifies that the responsible person is to make a check of some kind in order to see if a particular obligation is being kept. This check is accomplished through the personal visitation of the ordinary or through periodical reports as demanded of the vicars forane or of the pastors themselves. The obligation to see that sacred missions are held is placed upon bishops since they are the chief pastors in their respective dioceses. It is their duty to see that the faith and morals of their people are protected.[20]

B. Obligation of the Pastors

The obligation of seeing that sacred missions are held is placed both upon the bishops and the pastors. The obligation of the bishop is more than one of vigilance for he holds the principal preaching office in his diocese; the pastors act as his assistants in fulfilling this obligation. If the pastor is not able to fulfill this obligation then the bishop must supply the need. If the pastor refuses or neglects to fulfill the obligation, the bishop is to send missionaries into the parish anyway.[21]

Pastors and those who are equal in law to pastors [22] are bound by the obligation stated in canon 1349. Therefore, all who are bound *ex officio* to provide for the care of souls, whether they are pastors of a parish in the strict canonical sense, or of a quasi-parish, or of a filial parish, are included.[23] Quasi-pastors in missionary territories could of course avail themselves of any relaxation which in this law the Holy See may have granted to their ordinaries.

Before the Code there was no obligation in common law to hold sacred missions.[24] Missions, however, were so highly recommended

[19] Cf. Cann. 253, § 2; 267, § 1, 2°; 336, § 2; 469; 842; 1261, § 1; 1357, § 2; 1478; 1519, § 1.

[20] Can. 336, § 2.

[21] Can. 1327, § 2; S.C. Ep. et Reg., *Senen.*, 23 iul. 1694.

[22] Can. 451.

[23] McVann, p. 151.

[24] Wernz-Vidal, *Ius Canonicum ad Codicis normam exactum* (7 vols. in 8, Romae: Universitas Gregoriana, 1923-1938), Vol. IV, Pars II, 63.

by various Popes [25] that it was considered imprudent for a pastor not to hold sacred missions for his people, even though he may not have been bound by a universal or any particular law to do so. The attitude of the Church in general followed the opinion of St. Alphonsus Liguori, who declared that a good pastor would not let four or five years pass without a mission.[26] This attitude was manifested in particular legislation before the Code [27], and has now been carried into the legislation of the Code. Sacred missions are so important for the spiritual welfare of the faithful that a definite obligation is indicated with a view to making sure that pastors will provide for sacred missions just as they must provide for other spiritual needs of their flocks.

Article 3. Extent of the Obligation

A. Universal Obligation for Parishes of the Latin Church

The obligation of holding sacred missions binds only in parishes or quasi-parishes in the Latin Church. Parishes in the Oriental rites are not bound by this obligation.[28] All types of parishes are included under the obligation, whether they are territorial, national, or personal. Canon 1349, § 2, states: "*Parochus, etiam religiosus, in his missionibus instituendis mandatis Ordinarii loci stare debet.*" All pastors, whether secular or religious, and regardless of his status of exemption as a religious, are bound to hold sacred missions in their parishes, and to obey their local ordinaries in any directions which they may give about the manner in which they are to be held. If any pastor fails to fulfill this obligation, the ordinary can send missionaries into the parish to provide sacred missions for the faithful.[29] The power of the ordinary to send missionaries into a parish, in the event that a pastor fails to provide sacred missions, is not stated explicitly in canon 1349, § 2. The possession of this

[25] E.g., Benedictus XIV, bulla *Gravissimum,* 8 sept. 1745—*Bull. Benedicti XIV,* I, 555-560; Pius VI, const. *Auctorem fidei,* 28 aug. 1784—*Fontes,* n. 475; Pius IX, ep. encycl. *Nostis et Nobiscum,* 8 dec. 1849—*Fontes,* n. 508.

[26] *Homo Apostolicus,* Tract. VII, n. 31, p. 144.

[27] E.g., the Provincial Council of Ravenna (1865)—*Coll. Lac.,* VI, 187.

[28] Can. 1.

[29] S.C. Ep. et Reg., *Senen,* 23 iul. 1694—*Fontes,* n. 1816.

power is to be understood in accordance with the principle of interpretation as indicated in canon 6, for according to the earlier law, now again enacted in the Code, the ordinary did indeed possess this power.[80]

B. Decennial Obligation for Parishes of the Latin Church

According to canon 1349, § 1, sacred missions are to be held *at least* every ten years. The irreducible minimum of the obligation is indicated. The use of the word *saltem* in texts of the pre-Code law indicated that the legislator wished to prevent all undue postponement in important matters.[81] Throughout the Code also, when the word *saltem* is used the superior may use his discretion in making the obligation even stricter.[82] The ordinary cannot without the permission of the Holy See extend the time for the fulfillment of the obligation of holding sacred missions, for in doing so he would be acting contrary to the Code. He can, however, decree that missions be held every year, or at other recurring periods of less than ten years, according as his discretion will suggest. Plenary and provincial councils and diocesan synods may pass laws which would require sacred missions to be held oftener than every ten years.[83]

It is important to note that, since the word *saltem* is used in canon 1349, § 1, any particular laws in force before the Code, which required missions to be held more often than every ten years, are still in force unless they have been abrogated by the proper superior. In every diocese, then, any particular legislation regarding sacred missions must be taken into account if one is to determine the exact character of the obligation relative to the holding of sacred missions.

[80] S.C. Ep. et Reg., *Senen.*, 23 iul. 1694: "Questi Emi miei Signori, udita l'istanza di V. S., che supplicava a darsele facoltà di poter mandare liberamente nelle Chiese curate dei Regolari li Missionari a predicare, e far altre funzioni, non estante, che dalli Parochi Regolari si pretenda d'impedirlo satto pretesto d'esenzione, mi hanno commandato di scriverle, ch'Ella può mandare li detti Missionarii nelle predette Chiese, anche coll'autorità di questa S. Congregazione. Glielo significo ec.—*Fontes*, n. 1816.

[81] Sebastianelli, *Praelectiones Iuris Canonici* (3 vols., Vol. I, *De Personis*, 2. ed. emendata et aucta, Romae: Pustet, 1905), I, 157.

[82] E.g., cann. 126; 130, § 2; 343, § 1.

[83] Wernz-Vidal, *Ius Canonicum*, Vol. IV, Pars II, 64.

CHAPTER VII

THE OBLIGATION OF HOLDING SACRED MISSIONS AS STATED IN PARTICULAR LEGISLATION

ARTICLE 1. SOURCE OF THE OBLIGATION

A. Authority of Plenary and Provincial Councils

A plenary council consists in the convocation of all of the bishops in a certain country or part of the world, while a provincial council comprises only the bishops of a single province. The authority of these councils rests upon their review and recognition by the Holy See. Even before the Code, plenary and provincial councils submitted their decrees to Rome for recognition. This procedure became part of the universal law of the Church in the year 1588.[1]

The authority for plenary and provincial councils under the Code also rests upon the Holy See. Permission for convoking a plenary council must be obtained from the Pope, who appoints a legate to preside over the council.[2] The metropolitan of the province convokes and presides over a provincial council. If he is lawfully impeded or if the archepiscopal see is vacant, then the senior suffragan bishop in the province takes his place.[3]

The laws of both plenary and provincial councils are not to be promulgated until the Holy See has examined the acts and decrees of the respective councils. The manner of their promulgation and the time when they are to become effective are determined by the council itself; and the laws are thereafter obligatory in the entire territory.[4]

The jurisdictional powers of plenary and provincial councils

[1] Sixtus V, bulla *Immensa aeterni,* 22 ian. 1588—*Bull. Rom. Taur.,* VII, 991.

[2] Can. 281.

[3] Can. 284.

[4] Can. 291.

are derived from the Code. The laws passed by these councils exceed episcopal power, for an individual bishop cannot legislate for any territory other than his own.[5] Plenary and provincial decrees have force over the whole country or province, even over the bishops who constitute the council.[6] The ordinaries cannot dispense from plenary or provincial laws except in particular cases and for a just cause.[7]

B. Authority of Synods

The diocesan synod consists in an official meeting of the bishop of a diocese with the dignitaries of the diocese, the pastors of the city in which the synod is held, at least one pastor from each rural deanery, religious superiors, and others whom the bishop may wish to invite.[8] The bishop, however, is the sole legislator in the synod, the others having only a consultative vote; he alone attaches any authoritative signature to the synodal constitutions. If the decrees are promulgated in the synod, they become obligatory at once, unless express provision is made to the contrary.[9] Copies of the synodal constitutions are often sent to Rome for the Vatican archives, but such procedure is not required by law.[10]

Article 2. Nature of the Obligation

A. Obligation of the Bishops

If a plenary or provincial council orders that sacred missions be held oftener than the time specified by the Code, then all the bishops affected by the decrees of such a council would be bound

[5] Can. 291, § 2; S.C.S. Off., instr. 10 sept. 1876, ad 1, 2—*Fontes,* n. 484.

[6] Murphy, *Legislative Powers of the Provincial Council,* The Catholic University of America Canon Law Studies, n. 257 (Washington, D. C.: The Catholic University of America Press, 1947), p. 76.

[7] Can. 291, § 2.

[8] Can. 358.

[9] Can. 362.

[10] For a more complete treatment of the diocesan synod, confer Donnelly, *The Diocesan Synod,* The Catholic University of America Canon Law Studies, n. 74 (Washington, D. C.: The Catholic University of America, 1932).

to enforce the law. Synodal laws would not be allowed to run contrary to the higher laws.

Before the Code, some provincial councils placed the obligation upon bishops to see that sacred missions were held at regular intervals.[11] Other councils left the time and manner of holding missions to the discretion of the ordinaries.[12] Some councils placed the responsibility on both bishops and pastors to see that sacred missions were held.[13] Sacred missions were ordered to be held by a number of councils which did not specifically place the responsibility upon the bishops or upon the pastors, but the obligation rested of course upon the bishops, for it was they who had to see that the decrees of the councils were carried out in their respective dioceses.[14]

Since many councils did not impose the holding of sacred missions as a strict obligation, but merely urged that they be held if at all possible, the bishops who were affected by the decrees of these councils were left free, before the Code, in their discretion to make them obligatory in their dioceses or to let them stand without any strictly binding force.[15]

B. Obligation of the Pastors

Pastors themselves were directly obliged by some councils to hold sacred missions.[16] Occasionally a council placed the obligation

[11] E.g., Urbino (1859)—*Coll. Lac.*, VI, 69-70; Strigonia (1858)—*op. cit.*, V, 76.

[12] E.g., Westminster I (1852)—*op. cit.*, III, 942; Thurles (1850)—*op. cit.*, III, 767; Cashel (1853)—*op. cit.*, III, 829.

[13] E.g., Australia II (1895)—*Acta et Decreta Concilii Plenarii Australiensis II, anno 1895*, decr. 263.

[14] E.g., Naples (1699)—*Coll. Lac.*, I, 255; Pisa (1850)—*op. cit.*, VI, 238; Loreto (1850)—*op. cit.*, VI, 800-809; Meeting of Austrian Bishops (1856)—*op. cit.*, V, 124; Vienna (1858)—*op. cit.*, V, 186.

[15] E.g., National Synod of Hungary (1882)—*op. cit.*, V, 938; Bavaria (1848)—*op. cit.*, V, 1211; Auch (1851)—*op. cit.*, IV, 174; Rheims (1851)—*op. cit.*, IV, 1203; Dublin (1853)—*op. cit.*, V, 811-862; Tuam (1854)—*op. cit.*, III, 862; Venice (1859)—*op. cit.*, VI, 323; Cologne (1860)—*op. cit.*, V, 371; Calocza (1863)—*op. cit.*, V, 713; Second Council of the English, Dutch, and Danish Colonies (1867)—*op. cit.*, III, 1114; Plenary Council of Latin American countries (1899)—*Acta et Decreta Concilii Plenarii Americae Latinae*, n. 699; Cincinnati II (1858)—*Coll. Lac.*, III, 210.

[16] E.g., Bordeaux (1850)—*Coll. Lac.*, I, 602; Aix (1850)—*op. cit.*, I,

upon all those who were entrusted with the care of souls.[17] Pastors were obliged to provide sacred missions distinct from other parochial functions. In other words, a pastor could not call the *Forty Hours' Devotion*, Lenten devotions, or any other required service a sacred mission and thus fulfill the obligation.[18]

Many synods followed the lead of the provincial councils, and either repeated the directions of the councils on sacred missions or ordered a more specific time relative to the interval between missions in a parish.[19]

Article 3. Extent of the Obligation

A. Its Binding Character in all the Parishes of the Diocese or Province

All parishes, regardless of whether they are ruled by the religious or the secular clergy, are bound by the provincial and the synodal laws concerning sacred missions, just as they are bound by the laws of the Code. Particular legislation before and after the Code has been duly cognizant of the instruction of the Holy See, which acknowledged for bishops the power to send missionaries into a parish in order to provide sacred missions for the faithful.[20] The II Plenary Council of Baltimore (1866), provides a good example to show that bishops were fully aware of this power.[21]

As a rule, national and personal parishes are bound by the

1002, 1020; Bourges (1850)—*op. cit.*, I, 1128; Prague (1860)—*op. cit.*, V, 480; Utrecht (1865)—*op. cit.*, V, 882.

[17] E.g., Albi (1850)—*op. cit.*, IV, 430.

[18] McVann, p. 152.

[19] E.g., Paderborn (1867)—*AKKR*, XV (1867), 99; Ponticherry (1844)—*Coll. Lac.*, III, 655; Smyrna (1869)—*op. cit.*, VI, 573; Boston (1868)—*Constitutiones Dioecesanae II Synodi Dioecesis Bostonensis*, n. 216.

[20] S.C. Ep. et Reg., *Senen.*, 23 iul. 1694—*Fontes*, n. 1816.

[21] ". . . Ubicunque ab Ordinariis constituti fuerint hujusmodi Missionarii, pastores animarum in Domino hortamur, ut illorum ministerii beneficia suis ovibus procurent tempore opportuno. Si vero unquam pastorem aliquem hac in re suo officio deesse contigerit, ab Episcopus cogendus erit ad Missionarios accersendos; quod si non fecerit, ipse Episcopus eos mittat."—*Coll. Lac.*, III, 525-526.

provincial and synodal laws on sacred missions. There is an indication in some particular legislation, however, that a relaxation of the law is sometimes granted when it is difficult to obtain priests who speak the language of the people in a particular parish.[22]

An interesting contrast can be noticed in the legislation of some councils and synods about the relative need of sacred missions in the cities and thickly-populated districts and in the rural sections. Some made the obligation quite strict for the cities, but were willing to make allowances for country parishes.[23] Others believed that the rural districts were the most neglected, and therefore needed the benefit of sacred missions before the cities.[24] The different nationalities and classes of people in a diocese were provided for with special sacred missions by some particular legislation.[25]

These various additional prescriptions about sacred missions in conciliar and synodal legislation are valid as long as there is observed the fundamental obligation expressed in canon 1349, which requires missions to be held in every parish at least every ten years. The Holy See, of course, by approval of conciliar legislation or by indult could allow a relaxation or change in the law.

B. The Various Times for the Fulfillment of the Obligation

Since, as has already been noted, the use of the word *saltem* in canon 1349 allows councils and synods to make the obligation of holding sacred missions even more exacting, there are considerable differences in the times specified for the fulfillment of the obligation. It makes no difference whether the councils or synods were held before or after the Code, their decrees on sacred missions are still in effect as long as they have not been revoked or supplanted by subsequent legislation, and as long as they are not contrary to the

[22] E.g., Mount Lebanon (1736)—*op. cit.*, II, 103-106; Tarragona (1727) —*op. cit.*, I, 326; Quito (1869)—*op. cit.*, VL, 436.

[23] E.g., Vienna (1858)—*op. cit.*, V, 186; Urbino (1859)—*op. cit.*, VI, 323.

[24] E.g., National Synod of Hungary (1822)—*op. cit.*, V, 938.

[25] E.g., for the colored, Baltimore II (1866), Tit. X, cap. 4, n. 488—*op. cit.*, III, 531; for Mexicans, *Synodus Dioecesana Dallasensis, anno 1927*, n. 50; for various classes of parishioners, *Acta et Decreta Synodi Dioecesanae Quebecensis Secundae, anno 1940*, decr. 403.

Code provision of holding sacred missions at least every ten years.[26]

Many councils and synods prescribe the same obligation which the Code prescribes for they simply repeat the words of the Code.[27] In some dioceses sacred missions must be held every seven years.[28] A great number of councils and synods ordered sacred missions to be held in the parishes every five years.[29] Some dioceses ordered

[26] Wernz-Vidal, *Ius Canonicum*, Vol. IV, Pars II, 64.

[27] E.g., the following councils are cited by McVann on pages 151 to 153: *Concilium Plenarium Siculum, Panormi anno habitum* [Sicily], can. 26; *Concilium Provinciale Hispalense, anno 1924* [Seville, Spain], can. 260; *Concilium Plenarium Lusitanum, anno 1926* [Portugal], can. 413; *Concilium II Provinciale Vallisoletanum, anno 1930* [Valladolid, Spain], decr. 272; *Concilium Plenarium Aemilianae et Flaminiae Regionis, Bononiae anno 1932 habitum* [Northern Central Italy], decr. 32. Cf. also the following councils and synods: *Acta et Decreta Concilii Provincialis Tuamensis, anno 1933,* n. 30; *Estatutos Sinodales de la Diocesis de San Cristobal, Venuezuela, 1936,* stat. 648-650; *Synodus Dioecesana Cincinnatensis Quarta, anno 1920,* n. 32; *Statutes of the Diocese of Crookston Promulgated at the First Synod of Crookston, 1921,* n. 396; *Decreta Synodi Dioecesanae Mobiliensis Tertiae, anno 1921,* n. 75; *I Synodus Altunensis, anno 1922,* n. 85; *Statuta Dioecesana Synodi Quartae Leavenworthensis, anno 1922,* n. 195; *Statutes of the Diocese of Wheeling Promulgated at the Diocesan Synod, 1923,* n. 338; *Synodus Wayne Castrensis, anno 1927,* can. 31; *Montereyensis-Fresnensis Synodus Prima, anno 1929,* n. 93; *Synodus Dioecesana Cajetana Sexta, anno 1934,* constit. 25.

[28] E.g., *Acta et Decreta Provincialis Mechliniensis IV,* anno 1927, n. 211.

[29] E.g., *Acta et Decreta Concilii Plenarii Episcoporum Hiberniae, apud Maynutiam, anno 1927,* decr. 375; *Acta Concilii Plenarii Pedemontani, Taurini, anno 1927,* can. 14 (cited by McVann on page 151); *Decreta Concilii Provincialis Toletani, anno 1930,* decr. 313 (cited by McVann on page 151; *Acta et Decreta Synodi Dioecesanae Quebecensis Secundae, anno 1940,* decr. 403; and in the United States the following synods: *Statuta Dioecesana IV Synodi Pittsburgensis, anno 1920,* n. 209; *Nova Aureliae Synodus Sexta, anno 1922,* n. 261; *Constitutiones Dioecesanae Natchensis, anno 1922,* n. 261; *Dioecesana Synodus Alexandriae, anno 1924,* n. 14; *Synodus Dioecesana Brooklyniensis Quinta, anno 1926,* n. 45; *Statuta Dioecesana Angelorum et Sancti Didaci Synodus Quinta, anno 1927,* n. 184; *Synodus Dioecesana Dallasensis Secunda, anno 1927,* n. 50; *Statuta Dioecesana Ogdensburgensis XIII Synodus, anno 1928,* n. 54; *Statuta Dioecesana Lacus Salsi Prima, anno 1929,* n. 183; *Synodus Dioecesana Sancti Ludovici, anno 1929,* n. 146; *Synodus Dioecesana Richmondiensis Tertia, anno 1932,* n. 178; *Third Synod of Davenport, 1932,* n. 55; *Synodus Dioecesana Omahensis Quarta, anno 1934,* n. 338; *Synodus Roffensis Quinta, anno 1935,* n. 37; *Synodus Trentonensis Tertia, anno 1936,* n. 266;

sacred missions to be held every three or four years.[30] Other dioceses made it mandatory to hold sacred missions every three years.[31] And both before and after the Code some dioceses ordered sacred missions to be held every two years or even annually.[32]

Statuta Dioecesis Bellevillensis, V Synodus, anno 1939, n. 186 *Acta et Decreta Synodi Primae Toletanae in America, anno 1943,* n. 291; *Constitutions of the Diocese of Lafayette, La., 1943,* n. 283; *Synodus Archidioeceseos Indianapolitanae (I) Septima, anno 1947,* n. 115; *Statutes of the Diocese of Pueblo, First Diocesan Synod, 1948,* stat. 256.

[30] E.g., *Synodus Dioecesana Albanensis Tertia, anno 1884,* n. 27; *Synodus Dioecesis Buffalensis, anno 1886,* tit. XIV; *Synodus Dioecesanae Neo-Eboracensis Quinta, anno 1886,* n. 42; *Constitutiones VI Synodi Dioecesis Bostoniensis, anno 1919,* n. 152; *Synodus Dioecesana Syracusensis Undecima, anno 1921,* n. 42.

[31] E.g., *Constitutiones Dioecesanae Synodi Septimae Decimae Carolopolitanae, anno 1925,* n. 190; *Synodus Dioecesana Elpasensis Prima, anno 1930,* n. 20; *Acta et Decreta Concilii Provincialis in Oregon IV, anno 1932,* decr. 38; *Statuta Dioecesis Savannensis-Atlantensis, anno 1939,* n. 132; *Synodus Dioecesana Fargensis Prima, anno 1941,* n. 527.

[32] E.g., Naples (1699)—*Coll. Lac.,* I, 255; *Statuta Archidioecesana Synodi Secundae Sancti Francisci, anno 1936,* n. 343.

CHAPTER VIII

THE FULFILLMENT OF THE OBLIGATION OF HOLDING SACRED MISSIONS

Article 1. Preparations for Sacred Missions

A. Permission of the Local Ordinary

No one is permitted to preach in public unless he has received a canonical mission or authorization from a lawful superior either by special faculty or by appointment to an office to which the duty of preaching is attached by the sacred canons.[1] The local ordinary is the only one who can grant the faculty to preach for his own territory, both to members of the secular clergy and to non-exempt religious.[2] Exempt religious must obtain the faculty to preach from the local ordinary if they are preaching to others than to members of their own community or household.[3] The local ordinary must not deny the preaching faculty to religious presented by their superior, or recall a faculty once granted, unless he have a serious reason for so doing.[4] Religious are not allowed without the permission of their superiors to make use of their faculty for preaching.[5]

When a pastor, secular or religious, plans to hold a sacred mission in his parish, he should first obtain the necessary faculties for the missionaries from the local ordinary. If the missionaries who are to give the sacred mission already have the diocesan faculties for preaching, there is no strict obligation in law which would demand any further permission.[6] Even if there were no particular legislation

[1] Can. 1328.

[2] Can. 1337.

[3] Can. 1338, § 2.

[4] Can. 1339, § 1.

[5] Can. 1339, § 2.

[6] Cocchi, *Commentarium in Codicem Iuris Canonici*, Vol. VI (3. ed., Taurinorum Augustae: ex Officina Libraria Marietti, 1933), 56.

which requires the obtaining of this permission for those who already have the faculty for preaching, it would still be most advisable for the pastor to notify the ordinary about those who are to give the mission, as also about the contemplated dates for the mission. The ordinary has full power to regulate sacred missions in any way he sees fit, and all pastors must abide by his decisions in the matter.[7]

With reference to secular or religious priests from outside the diocese, pastors should refrain from inviting them to preach in their parishes until they have first obtained permission from the ordinary of the place where the sacred mission is to be given.[8] The reason for obtaining this permission beforehand from the bishop is fairly obvious. A particular missionary may be a *persona non grata* to a bishop, for in previous missions which he has given he may have acquired a reputation of being flamboyant or eccentric in his methods of preaching, and imprudent or erroneous in the doctrines which he preached. The bishop is the duly constituted protector of faith and morals in a diocese, and he has a solemn obligation to protect the faithful against scandal and error. If a missionary is unkown to the ordinary of the place, the bishop should not grant the permission to preach until he has received from the priest's ordinary a favorable report concerning the knowledge, piety, and good character of the preacher.[9]

The faculty for preaching is to be regularly given only to priests and deacons.[10] If a cardinal should be invited to preach, no permission is needed from the local ordinary, for cardinals enjoy the faculty of preaching the word of God everywhere.[11] Bishops also enjoy this privilege of cardinals as long as the local ordinary is not actively opposed to their preaching in the diocese.[12]

It is important to make sure that any permission for preaching a sacred mission should also contain faculties for the hearing of confessions. One of the principal objectives of a mission is to arouse

[7] Can. 1349, § 2.
[8] Can. 1341.
[9] Can. 1341, § 1.
[10] Can. 1342.
[11] Can. 239, § 1, 3°.
[12] Can. 349, § 1, 1°.

sinners to repentance and the devout to greater devotion. Opportunity, then, should be given to the faithful to go to confession to the missionary priests rather than to their own parish priests, so that they may have perfect freedom of conscience. Missionaries, during the time of a sacred mission, may absolve, *ipso iure*, those sins which the ordinary has reserved to himself.[13]

If the permission to preach a sacred mission were granted, but not the faculties to hear confessions, one of the principal purposes of the mission would be defeated.[14] The ordinary, however, is bound to make sure before he grants the faculty to hear confessions that the recipient is worthy and capable of such trust.[15] The ordinary can dispense from the examination given before the bestowal of confessional faculties if he considers the missionary, from his reputation, as being capable, or if he has obtained sufficient information in the inquiry made previous to the granting of the preaching faculty.[16]

In order that the reception of the sacrament of penance may not be rendered odious, preachers of retreats and missions are warned by the Holy Office not to mention in the pulpit, even indirectly, anything protected by the seal of confession.[17]

In the United States bishops, in virtue of their Quinquennial Faculties, can dispense from certain impediments at the time of a sacred mission. The impediments concerned are: (1) consanguinity in the second or third degree touching the first, provided that there be no scandal or wonderment arising from the use of the faculty in this regard; (2) consanguinity in the second degree of the collateral line; (3) affinity in the first degree of the collateral line; and (4) public decency in the first degree, provided that there be no doubt that one of the parties is not the offspring of the other. Although canon 1349 states that sacred missions should be given at least once in ten years, they may be given oftener, and as often

[13] Can. 899, § 3.

[14] McVann, p. 151.

[15] Can. 877.

[16] Cann. 1341, § 1; 877, § 1.

[17] S.C.S. Off. instr., 9 iun. 1915—*Il Monitore Ecclesiastico* (Romae, 1876—), XLI (1917), 200.

as they are given the faculty to dispense from the impediments enumerated above can be used. Dispensations can be granted in virtue of this faculty only in those cases in which the parties are actually living in concubinage. This condition is necessary for the valid use of the faculty.[18]

B. Circumstances of Time and Place

The Code is silent about the circumstances relating to sacred missions, except for noting that the bishop is free to impose certain rules, which when imposed are to be obeyed.[19] The bishop, for example, may designate the number of missionaries, the topics to be treated, the length of the mission, the suitable times, and the proper places for the missions.

St. Alphonsus Liguori urged that missions should last five weeks.[20] Today, however, a sacred mission lasts regularly for one week. Missions lasting two weeks—one week for the men and one for the women—or even a longer time in very large parishes are also common. Sometimes a mission for the children is given in the afternoon for approximately three days while the mission for the adults is still in progress. Generally two missionaries alternate in giving the various exercises of the mission.[21]

The essential features of the mission are the daily attendance at Mass and frequent reception of Holy Communion, and the participation in the evening services, which usually include the Rosary, a sermon, and Benediction. The apostolic blessing is given at the end of the mission. The sermon topics for a mission are similar to those for a retreat, e. g., perseverance, the last things, sin.[22] Mis-

[18] Eagleton, *The Diocesan Quinquennial Faculties Formula IV* (The Catholic University of America Canon Law Studies, n. 248, Washington, D. C.: The Catholic University of America Press, 1948), pp. 82-83.

[19] Can. 1349, § 2.

[20] *The Complete Ascetical Works of Saint Alphonsus,* XV, 73-74.

[21] Hennrich, "Concerning Parish Missions"—*The Homiletic and Pastoral Review* (New York, 1900—), XLIII (1942), 182-183 (hereafter cited *Hom. & Pas. Rev.*).

[22] Cf. series of articles on sacred missions—*AER,* II (1890), 86, 92, 161, 173, 178, 191, 193, 194, 196, 208.

sionaries often consult the pastors of the parishes in which they are to preach in order to determine the subjects which may be the most applicable. Sometimes specific recommendations are made in particular legislation.[23]

The Code does not specify any particular time of the year for the fulfillment of the obligation of holding sacred missions. Numerous suggestions, however, about the best time for holding sacred missions have been made in particular legislation. The Provincial Council of Naples (1699), which was the first council to make sacred missions obligatory, urged that missions be held in the parishes just before the visitation of the bishop, so that the parish might be spiritually as well as temporally in good order.[24] The II Plenary Council of Baltimore (1866), suggested as fitting times for the giving of sacred missions: the seasons of Advent and Lent, the occasions of First Communion and of Confirmation, and the time immediately preceding the episcopal visitation.[25] The bishops could make obligatory the specific times of the year for the holding of sacred missions. There is no recorded instance of any strict obligation for the holding of sacred missions at any particular time or season of the year; at most the councils or synods made some recommendations.

There is no mention in either universal or particular legislation of the place for the holding of sacred missions. The church is the customary place for holding sacred missions, particularly since daily Mass, the reception of Holy Communion, and Benediction are integral features of the mission. There is no reason, however, why the bishop could not allow the mission to be held in some other fitting place for a just cause, such as that of accommodating larger crowds than the church can hold.[26]

[23] E.g., sermons on temperance, Baltimore III (1886)—*Acta et Decreta Concilii Plenarii Baltimorensis III*, n. 260; sermons on hell, Latin American Countries (1899)—*Acta et Decreta Concilii Plenarii Americae Latinae*, decr 705.

[24] *Coll. Lac.*, I, 255.

[25] *Op. cit.*, III, 525-526, decree n. 473.

[26] Berutti, *Institutiones Iuris Canonici*, Vol. IV (Taurini-Romae: Marietti, 1940), 363-364.

The local ordinary can, if he deems it necessary, forbid sacred missions to be held in his diocese during a special emergency. Such an emergency might arise from a conflict with the civil authorities or from the necessity of avoiding large crowds in time of war or epidemic.[27] Should the period of emergency extend beyond ten years, a dispensation should be obtained from the Holy See, since no power is given to the bishop to dispense from the law of holding sacred missions other than that which he might obtain through canons 15 or 81.

Article 2. Use of Priests from Outside of the Parish

A. The Secular and the Religious Clergy

The Code does not mention who are to be entrusted with the work of conducting the sacred missions. The mind of the Church, however, as expressed in the declarations of the Holy See previous to the Code [28], and also in particular legislation [29], indicates that they should be priests who are from outside of the parish in which the sacred mission is to be given.

The reasons for such an attitude can easily be explained. No matter how competent the pastor and his assistants may be, the use of priests who are new to the parish adds interest to the mission, and larger numbers of the faithful are attracted to the mission from this human consideration alone. Better results can be obtained, also, through the use of missionaries who are trained especially for the work of sacred missions.

Most important of all, the use of outside priests affords greater freedom of conscience and is conducive to confidential interviews both in and outside of the confessional. Many parishioners, as a result of some past misunderstanding or from fear of embarrassment,

[27] Wernz-Vidal, *Ius Canonicum,* Vol. IV, Pars II, 63.

[28] Benedictus XIV, bulla *Gravissimum,* 8 sept. 1745—*Bull. Benedicti XIV,* I, 555-560; Pius IX, ep. encycl. *Nostis et Nobiscum,* 8 dec. 1849—*Fontes,* n. 508; Pius IX, ep. encycl. *Singulari quidem,* 17 mart. 1856—*op. cit.,* n. 521.

[29] E.g., Aix (1850)—*Coll. Lac.,* IV, 1020; Cashel (1853)—*op. cit.,* III, 829; Baltimore II (1866)—*op. cit.,* III, 526.

are reluctant to discuss personal problems with the priests who know them, and the occasion of a sacred mission, given by outside priests, affords them an excellent chance to get the help and the advice they so badly need.

Both the secular and religious clergy have been proficient in the work of sacred missions. There is no reason to indicate that one is to be preferred to the other, even though some authors have indicated that sacred missions are generally given by religious.[80] No preference is given in either the universal or the particular legislation. The problem generally resolves itself into the question of deciding who are available and competent for undertaking the work of sacred missions in a certain locality.

Religious, at the present time, make up the majority of those who are engaged in the work of sacred missions. The rôle of the secular clergy, however, has been very important in giving sacred missions, particularly in the formation of permanent diocesan missionary bands. Pope Benedict XIV praised the work done by the diocesan missionary bands in Naples and he urged the universal Church to follow that example.[81]

On the *agenda* of the Vatican Council (1869-1870), before it so abruptly came to an end, was a proposal submitted by the bishops of the Province of Naples that a band of priests be trained and appointed to give sacred missions for every diocese.[82] This proposal has never been acted upon, although it was given careful consideration at the time it was made.

Various particular councils recommended diocesan missionary bands.[83] The II Plenary Council of Baltimore (1866), strongly urged that a band of missionaries be established in each diocese: ". . . Valde animarum saluti promovendae prodesset si in unaquaque

[80] E.g., Claeys-Bouuaert-Simenon, *Manuale Juris Canonici* (3 vols., Vol. II, 1931; Vols. I et III, 3. ed., 1930, Gaudae et Leodii: in Seminariis Gaudavensi et Liodiensi), III, 116.

[81] Bulla *Gravissimum,* 8 sept. 1745—*Bull. Benedicti XIV,* I, 555-560.

[82] *Postulata Episcoporum Neapolitanorum,* Cap. III, xxviii—*Coll. Lac.,* VII, 810a.

[83] E.g., Bishops of Bavaria at Würzburg (1848)—*Coll. Lac.,* V, 1246b; Dublin (1853)—*op. cit.,* III, 811; Tuam (1854)—*op. cit.,* III, 862; Baltimore II (1866)—*op. cit.,* III, 525-526.

dioecesi Missionarii instituerentur, quorum vel unicum vel saltem praecipuum officium esset *Missiones*, vel *exercitia spiritualia* statis temporibus per dioecesim congregationibus dare . . ."[34] As has already been seen, regulations of particular councils which are not contrary to the Code continue in force concerning sacred missions as long as they have not been revoked or supplanted. There arises then the question whether the II Plenary Council of Baltimore imposed a strict obligation upon bishops to organize diocesan missionary bands in their respective dioceses. Although the words used by this council throughout the treatise on sacred missions stress the necessity of holding missions and of having competent priests to carry on the work, nowhere can there be found a strict obligation to form diocesan missionary bands. The words, "*Valde animarum saluti promovendae podesset si in unaquaque dioecesi Missionarii instituerentur,*" imply a strong exhortation rather than a strict obligation. Naturally, the bishops were expected to carry out the recommendations of the council in their own dioceses, if at all possible. Most dioceses followed the lead of the Council of Baltimore and either established diocesan missionary bands or encouraged religious mission bands to do the work within their boundaries.[35]

In many instances diocesan missionary bands gradually developed into religious congregations or quasi-religious societies.[36] Other religious communities have made sacred missions an important part of their work.[37] Religious communities often differ widely in the

[34] *Op. cit.*, III, 525, decree n. 473.

[35] With the approval of the hierarchy in the United States, an Apostolic Mission House was established by the Paulists in 1903 at the Catholic University of America in Washington, D. C., for the purpose of training diocesan missionary bands. Priests were trained for missions to non-Catholics as well as for parochial missions. This house is no longer in existence, but the good effects remain in the number of trained diocesan missionaries throughout the United States. Outstanding among the diocesan missionary bands in America today are those in the Archdiocese of New York, Boston, Chicago, and San Francisco.

[36] E.g., the Vincentians, Redemptorists, Passionists, Precious Blood Fathers, Fathers of Mercy, Eudists.

[37] E.g., the Oblates of Mary Immaculate, the Holy Cross Fathers, the

non-essential features of sacred missions with reference to the methods used, the usual sermon topics employed, and the duration for which the missions are conducted. As a general rule, pastors are left free to choose any religious community they desire for the giving of the sacred missions. Restrictions are seldom placed upon them in this respect as long as the obligation of holding sacred missions is satisfactorily fulfilled.

B. Status of the Missionaries

A number of particular councils were concerned about the relationship of the missionaries to the pastor in the parish.[38] These councils wished to impress the missionaries with the fact that permission by the local ordinary to preach a sacred mission in a parish should not be construed in any way as impairing the authority and jurisdiction of the pastor. If the missionaries were sent by the bishop to preach a sacred mission against the will of the pastor, then the pastor could regulate only the incidental features of the mission, such as the time for Mass and the evening services. If the mission is given in a parish that has no parish priest, the ordinary usually grants the missionaries complete faculties to cover the situation.[39]

The II Plenary Council of Baltimore warned missionaries not to interfere with the internal affairs of the parish.[40] One of the favorite objections offered by pastors who were not in favor of sacred missions was that the missionaries undermined their authority and caused dissension in their parishes. Pastors, however, were

Franciscans, the Dominicans, the Jesuits, the Marists, the Carmelites, the Augustinians, the Benedictines, and the Paulists.

[38] E.g., Baltimore II (1866)—*Coll. Lac.*, III, 525-526; Australia II (1895) —*Acta et Decreta Concilii Plenarii Australiensis II, anno 1895*, decr. 263-269.

[39] E.g., *Estatutos Sinodales de la Diocesis de San Cristobal, Venezuela, anno 1936*, est. 647-650.

[40] ". . . Meminerint vero viri illi, qui ad Missionem vocantur, se in auxilium tantum Pastorum arcessiri. . . . In rebus autem quae paroeciae curam vel administrationem respiciunt, ne se immisceant. . . ."—*Coll. Lac.*, III, 526, decree n. 475.

urged to discuss with the missionaries in a friendly manner any difficulties which might arise from their presence in the parish.[41]

Several councils found it necessary to warn pastors and missionaries not to be over-zealous in trying to make the occasion of a sacred mission a profitable one temporally as well as spiritually.[42] These councils pointed out that serious scandal may be given to the faithful if there is an over-emphasis on obtaining money. Missions can be a great help in bringing back those who are weak in their faith, and therefore special care must be taken not to give them an excuse for staying away from the mission.

There is considerable particular legislation on the fees to be paid to the missionaries and other expenses connected with sacred missions.[43] Missionaries were warned not to offer for sale pamphlets, rosaries, medals, crucifixes, and the like without the consent of the pastor and the approval of the local ordinary.[44]

As a rule the instructions of the particular councils with regard to those who were entrusted with the work of giving sacred missions were not given as strict obligations but rather as strong exhortations.

41 ". . . Cum populo dum agunt, de eo quod laudandum est, disserant; quod ipsis censura dignum videtur, inconsulto Pastore discrete taceant. Si quid vero corrigendum ipsis occurrerit, comiter illud Pastori indicent ejusque audiant opinionem; vel, si necessarium iudicaverint, de re Episcopum certiorem faciant. Memores tamen sint *conditionis suae; et caveant ne inopportuno vel incauto zelo bonum, quod ex eorum laboribus provenire potest, vel praepediant, vel certe minuant. . . .*"—*op. cit.*, III, 526, decree n. 475.

42 Baltimore II (1866)—*Ibid.*, decree n. 476; *Acta et Decreta Concilii Plenarii Episcoporum Hiberniae, anno 1927,* decr. 372; *Concilii Venetii Provincialis II, anno 1928,* decr. 441 (cited by McVann on p. 153); *Concilii II Provincialis Vallisoletanum, anno 1930,* decr. 272 (cited by McVann on p. 153).

43 E.g., the II Plenary Council of Australia (1895) decreed that those giving sacred missions were to receive, apart from their expenses, a stipend of five pounds sterling each for every week.—*Acta et Decreta Concilii Plenarii Australiensis, anno 1895,* decreta 263, 267, 269. The V Synod of Seattle (1938) stated that the remuneration for a sacred mission should not be more than $100 a week without the expressed consent of the ordinary.—*Synodus Dioecesana Seattlensis Quinta, anno 1938,* stat. 81, n. 3. The I Synod of Fargo (1941) declared that household expenses at the time of the Forty Hours' Devotion or of a Mission are to be borne by the parish as long as they do not exceed $15 per day.—*Liber Synodalis Fargensis I, anno 1941,* stat. 401.

44 Baltimore II (1866)—*Coll. Lac.*, III, 526, decree n. 476.

Particular councils, for the most part, were reluctant to impose strict obligations with reference to the circumstances connected with sacred missions. The value of sacred missions was strongly emphasized, but the details were left to be worked out at the discretion of the local ordinaries. The various councils and synods believed that it was sufficient to insist upon the obligation of holding the sacred missions in the parishes within the stated intervals. In this respect the particular legislation follows the Code closely.

Article 3. Types of Sacred Missions

A. General Missions

Many dioceses have found general missions very beneficial. A general mission is one in which all the parishes of a diocese or of a certain district have missions in their churches at the same time. Such an arrangement has both advantages and disadvantages. General missions enable a diocese to achieve regularity and uniformity in giving missions. A diocesan-wide campaign can be launched to stir up interest in the mission, and greater crowds undoubtedly can be attracted because of the widespread publicity. A general mission is particularly beneficial in cities where parishioners are prone to change residence frequently.

The principal disadvantage, in a general mission, lies in the difficulty of obtaining a large number of capable missionaries at the same time.[45] Long and careful preparations are necessary if a general mission is to be a success. Missionaries must be contacted a year or two before the dates of the proposed general mission in order to make sure that a sufficient number can be obtained.[46]

Some dioceses have found it easier to arrange general missions for the cities and thickly-populated districts, and particular missions

[45] Recent newspaper reports indicate that this has proved quite a problem in England, where general missions are planned to be held throughout the country in the year 1949. Appeals have been made to America and other countries to supply missionaries for this project.

[46] Kassiepe, *Die katholische Volksmission in der neuen Zeit. Grundsätzliches und Praktisches für Seelsorger*, pp. 12-13.

for the rural sections.[47] It would be against the intention of the Code if a general mission were held in one place for all the parishioners coming together from several parishes, for canon 1349 indicates that each parish should have its own mission.

B. Particular Missions

In dioceses where particular missions are the general custom, the arrangements are generally left up to the pastor. Unless there is particular legislation that regulates features of the mission, the pastor is left free to select the time for the mission and to choose the missionaries. If possible, arrangements with the missionaries should be made at least six months before the time of the mission. Immediate preparations for the mission should be undertaken by the pastor through sermons and public notices about the coming mission. It is often advantageous to discuss with the missionaries beforehand what subjects need special attention in a particular parish.[48]

Some pastors find it advantageous to check the efficacy of a mission by having a special report made not only of the attendance at the services, but of the number of confessions heard and the number of Communions distributed. Since the enactment of the Code new ideas have been developed, particularly by the various religious communities engaged in this work, to increase the efficacy of sacred missions.[49]

[47] E.g., Naples (1699)—*Coll. Lac.*, I, 255; Urbino (1859)—*op. cit.*, VI, 69, 70.

[48] E.g., *Concilium Plenarium Lusitanum, anno 1926,* can. 413 (this Plenary Council of Portugal is cited by McVann, p. 152).

[49] Cf. Healy, "Need of Parochial Missions," *Hom. & Pas. Rev.*, XXI (1920), 177-181; González, "Les misiones parroquiales," *Sal Terrae* (Santander, 1912—), IX (1920), 120-132; Krull, "Parochial Missions," *ER*, LXIV (1921), 614-616; Kapistran, "Die Bedeutung der ausserordentlichen Seelsorge für die Pfarrei," *Theologisch-praktische Quartalschrift* (Linz, 1848—), LXXXI (1928), 37-50 (hereafter cited *ThPrQs*); Maroto, "Il dritto canonico e le missioni," *Il Pensitore Missione* (Romae, 1929—), I (1929), 20-26; Bogsrücker, "Über Volkmissionen und Seelsorgaushilfen," *ThPrQs*, LXXXV (1932), 370-375; Henze, "De nova missionum paroecialium forma," *Commentarium pro Religiosis* (Romae, 1920-1934; ab anno 1935: *Commentarium pro Religiosis et Missionariis*), XV (1934), 56-64.

One of the most novel developments in particular sacred missions since the Code has been a new form of mission intended particularly for large city parishes. Each parish is divided into sections or circles. Missions are given for each one of these sections in chapels or other approved places within the boundaries of the parish. Further division is made by separate missions for the men and for the women. In some places the sectional missions for the adults are preceded and ended with three-day missions for the children, given in the parish church. It takes three months or more to fully cover the parish. Following this method of "dividing and conquering," missionaries have reported considerable success, particularly in the countries of Germany, Austria, Holland, and Switzerland.[50]

These missions are often called *domestic* missions, since they are frequently held in the homes of some of the parishioners. The missionaries, previous to the mission, try to visit all the families, Catholic or mixed, within the section to talk over any troubles they may have and to encourage them to come to the mission. Although this type of mission means a tremendous amount of work, the results, as compiled in the reports submitted by the missionaries and the pastors of the parishes, show an impressive superiority over the ordinary parochial missions. From a canonical viewpoint, there is nothing to be said against this new form of missions as long as they are held in the parishes at least every ten years and have the approval of the local ordinaries.[51]

[50] Henze, "De nova missionum paroecialium forma," *Commentarium pro Religiosis,* XV (1934), 56-64.

[51] *Loc. cit.*

CHAPTER IX

THE ENFORCEMENT OF THE OBLIGATION OF HOLDING MISSIONS

Article 1. Authority for the Enforcement

A. The Holy See

In many matters bishops are left free to decide whether or not certain devotions or pious practices should be introduced into their dioceses. They can forbid innovations if they believe such things are not beneficial for their flocks, or if they feel that the time is not opportune for the introduction of new devotions.[1] They remain free to approve or reject these devotions until the Holy See has officially registered its approval or disapproval.

Although the introduction of sacred missions into the life of the Church was marked with a great deal of success, there was, naturally enough, some criticism of sacred missions by those who felt that no permanent benefits were to be derived from them. Many of the critics were imbued with the Jansenistic spirit, and they resented anything which they considered a novel and undignified addition to the devotions of the Church. These critics received a severe setback in the year 1745, when Pope Benedict XIV published the memorable bull *Gravissimum.*[2]

In this papal document the work of sacred missions was given the unqualified support of the Pope, who had been in personal contact with the work and had been deeply impressed with the results. Opponents of missions received their deathblow when Pope Pius VI condemned the Synod of Pistoia (1786). Sacred missions had been criticized in this synod as being an empty noise and as not leaving any real effect upon the people. The Pope officially condemned this particular statement of the synod on sacred mis-

[1] Can. 336, § 2.

[2] *Bull. Benedicti XIV,* I, 555-560.

sions by saying that the criticism of sacred missions was rash, evil-sounding, dangerous, and injurious to pious customs and to the spread of the word of God.[3]

This condemnation of a particular synod did not directly affect the universal Church, but it clearly showed the attitude of the Holy See toward any who condemned or publicly criticized sacred missions. With the promulgation of the Code, sacred missions have been officially approved and ordered for all the parishes in the Latin Church. Bishops are not free to accept or reject sacred missions, nor are they free to publicly criticize their work. They are obliged, under the authority of the Holy See, to see that the law governing sacred missions is obeyed in their dioceses. They are left free to regulate the incidental circumstances connected with sacred missions.[4] The official approval of sacred missions by the Holy See lifts missions from the rank of merely pious devotions and treats them as important means in achieving the Church's purpose, which is the salvation of souls.

The Holy See has a perfect right to enforce the law on sacred missions just as it has for any other ecclesiastical law established for the universal Church. Bishops who opposed sacred missions and refused to have them in their dioceses could be punished even to the extent of removal from office if their refusal is equivalent to contempt for laws of the Holy See.[5]

B. The Local Ordinaries

One of the principal duties of a bishop is to see that the laws of the Church are obeyed in his diocese.[6] He begins to exercise his authority when he takes canonical possession of his diocese.[7] Among the laws which the bishop is bound to uphold is the obligation enacted in canon 1349, which requires him to watch that pastors have sacred missions in their parishes at least every ten years. The bishop is fully empowered to use his authority and to send mission-

[3] Const. *Auctorem fidei*, 28 aug. 1794, ad LXV—*Fontes*, n. 475.

[4] Can. 1349, § 2.

[5] Can. 2331.

[6] Can. 336, § 2.

[7] Can. 334, § 2.

aries into the parishes of his diocese to preach sacred missions should the pastors be derelict in their duty. This power, as has already been noted, is warranted in the present through the medium of canon 6, which upholds as binding whatever in the nature of law has been derived unchanged from the earlier legislation.[8]

The vicar general, in the event that the bishop is impeded, the apostolic administrator, and also the diocesan administrator, are all fully qualified to enforce this obligation of holding sacred missions should it be necessary that coercion be invoked.[9]

Article 2. Checks on the Fulfillment of the Obligation

A. Written Reports

All bishops are bound to make a report to the Supreme Pontiff every five years on the state of the dioceses committed to their care.[10] This report follows a formula prescribed by the Sacred Consistorial Congregation [11], which outlines in detail the matters which must be reported. A special section in this formula deals with the preaching of the word of God.[12] The bishops are asked to report on how canons 1340-1347 are being observed in their dioceses, but there is no mention of the obligation of holding sacred missions as required by canon 1349. Since there is no other directive which requires bishops to report to the Holy See on the obligation of holding sacred missions, it may be safely said that such a report is not necessary. The Holy Father, of course, could ask for a special report, or could question bishops about the fulfillment of this obligation on the occasion of their *ad limina* visit to Rome.[13]

In canon 1349 ordinaries are ordered *to watch* that pastors hold sacred missions in their parishes. This obligation of vigilance can be fulfilled by bishops in many ways. One of the most common checks on the fulfillment of this obligation is made through the

[8] Can. 1349, § 2; S.C. Ep. et Reg., *Senen.*, 23 iul. 1694—*Fontes*, n. 1816.
[9] Cann. 429, § 1; 312; 438.
[10] Can. 340, § 1.
[11] *AAS*, X (1919), 487.
[12] Formula, cap. IV, n. 31—*ibid.*, p. 489.
[13] Can. 341, § 1.

annual report required from every parish, by particular law, in most of the dioceses. Generally the report is made by the pastor on standard forms provided by the diocese. On these forms it is often asked when the latest mission was held, and sometimes even more detailed information, such as the names of the missionaries, the length of the mission, and other pertinent facts, is sought. By requiring mention of the names of the missionaries, the ordinary can thus check to see if the proper preaching faculties were obtained.[14]

The bishop can, if he so desires, require that an individual report be made by the pastor shortly after the mission has closed in his parish.[15] The pastor could be required to describe in this report the success of the mission in detail, such as the approximate attendance, the number of Confessions heard, and the number of Holy Communions distributed, and to furnish also other relevant information.

Still another check on the fulfillment of the obligation of holding sacred missions can be made through the reports which must be submitted to the bishop by the vicars forane.[16] Diocesan forms can be used, and a special inquiry regarding sacred missions can be incorporated in these forms.

B. Personal Visits

One of the most effective checks on the holding of sacred missions can be made by the bishop through personal consultation with the pastors of his diocese at the time of the episcopal visitation. As has already been noted, some councils specifically urged or recommended that missions be held in preparation for the visitation by the bishop.[17]

Bishops are bound by the obligation of visiting partially or completely their whole dioceses at least every five years. The bishops are to perform this visitation personally or, if impeded, through

[14] Can. 1341.

[15] E.g., *Concilium Plenarium Lusitanum, anno 1926*, can. 412 (cited by McVann on page 151).

[16] Can. 449.

[17] E.g., Naples (1699)—*Coll. Lac.*, I, 217; Baltimore II (1866)—*op. cit.*, III, 525.

the vicar general or some other representative.[18] In the United States the III Plenary Council of Baltimore (1884), requires that the episcopal visitation be completed at least every three years.[19]

The bishop can examine his clergy concerning their various obligations, and he can examine pastors particularly concerning their parochial duties. Among these parochial obligations is that of providing sacred missions for the faithful.[20] Religious who are pastors as well as the seculars are subject to the episcopal visitation in matters pertaining to parochial discipline.[21] The check on sacred missions by the bishop when he makes his visitation can be undertaken by him directly in person or by means of the printed questionnaire which is filled out by the pastor at the time of the visitation.[22]

Such a questionnaire, listing the salient features of the visitation, is usually sent to the pastor some time before the visitation. The bishop then checks the questionnaire and makes any pertinent comments. Two copies are generally made so that both the diocesan and parochial archives may have a record of the visitation. Questions relating to the holding of sacred missions would inquire about the date of the latest mission, and review the observance of any and all diocesan regulations relative to the specified manner in which the mission was to be conducted.

At the time of his visitation the bishop may ask for the pastor's opinion regarding the success that accompanied the holding of the latest sacred mission. The bishop may want to know something about the ability of the missionaries and also about other relevant factors, for his knowledge regarding these matters will be of help to him when he is asked to grant the required preaching faculty in the future.[23] The bishop may also check, if he thinks it advisable, to see if the pastor co-operated with the missionaries in preparing

[18] Can. 343, § 1.

[19] *Acta et Decreta Baltimorensis Concilii Plenarii Tertii, anno 1884* (Baltimorae: Typis Ioannis Murphy et Sociorum, 1886), n. 14.

[20] Slafkosky, *The Canonical Episcopal Visitation of the Diocese* (The Catholic University of America, Canon Law Studies, n. 142, Washington, D. C.: The Catholic University of America Press, 1941), p. 130.

[21] Cann. 344, § 2; 631, § 1; 1261, § 2.

[22] E.g., *Acta et Decreta Concilii Provincialis Tuamensis, anno 1933,* n. 30.

[23] Can. 1341.

for the mission. He can do this by questioning the pastor and by checking any written records which may be required by particular law, such as the Sunday announcements book.

Article 3. The Penalties for Failure to Fulfill the Obligation

A. General Legislation

There is no specific penalty contained in the Code or in other universal legislation for failure to fulfill the obligation of holding sacred missions in parishes. The bishop's use of his right and power to send missionaries into a parish when the pastor has failed to provide sacred missions cannot be considered a penalty in the strict sense of the term.[24] An ecclesiastical penalty denotes the privation of some good, which privation is effected by the lawful authority and inflicted for the correction of the delinquent and the punishment of the crime.[25] It is true that there is a supplanting of the pastor's rights when the bishop sends missionaries into a parish, but the pastor is not deprived of any of his lawful rights nor is he being directly punished in any way. The measure is taken solely for the good of souls.

If on the occasion of his visitation of a parish the bishop finds that the prescription of the Code on giving of sacred missions is not being obeyed, he should ordinarily give a paternal admonition in private, reminding the pastor of the law, and suggesting that he hold a sacred mission in his parish as soon as possible. If the pastor thereupon failed to act after this paternal admonition, the bishop could impose penal remedies and penances without going beyond the limits of a paternal procedure. Any penalties which the bishop imposes should be concerned primarily with the correction of the abuse.[26]

Even though a law, such as the one that regulates the holding of sacred missions, does not automatically invoke the application

[24] S.C. Ep. et Reg., *Senen.*, 23 iul. 1694—*Fontes*, n. 1816.

[25] Can. 2215.

[26] Slafkosky, *The Canonical Episcopal Visitation of the Diocese*, pp. 143-145.

of a penal sanction in the event of a violation of the law, the legitimate superior can punish the violation of the law by means of a just penalty. This can be done, even apart from any previous threat of punishment, if the occasioned scandal or the special gravity of the transgression warrants such drastic interpretation. Otherwise the guilty person cannot be punished unless he was previously warned and threatened with a *latae* or *ferendae sententiae* penalty in the event of a transgression, and then nevertheless violated the law.[27]

Scandal could conceivably follow from a pastor's failure to hold sacred missions in a parish if it becomes known that he deliberately refrained from fulfilling his duty in this matter. His example could influence other pastors in their action, and thus occasion a similar neglect of this duty on their part. Through such neglect the faithful could lose sight of the importance of sacred missions, so that as an inevitable result the spiritual standards of the parish would be lowered. If private admonitions have not proved of any avail, then the bishop may discreetly feel that the infliction of some penalty has become necessary if the scandal is to be effectively counteracted and the authority of the Church is to be duly restored to its place of honor and respect.

Pastors can be removed from their parishes by the bishop, after the proper canonical procedure, if they seriously neglect or violate certain parochial duties.[28] The failure to hold sacred missions in a parish would in itself not suffice for a bishop to remove a pastor from his parish, for the obligation in question is nowhere included under the parochial duties whose violation can be punished in such a manner.

B. *Particular Legislation*

There are, in particular law, no recorded instances of the enactment of either *latae* or *ferendae sententiae* penalties for the failure to obey the regulations relative to the holding of sacred missions. As noted before, the moral obligation of a pastor to provide sacred missions regularly for his people was indeed stressed, but no specific regulations of a penal character were ever invoked as a means for

[27] Can. 2222, § 1.

[28] Cann. 467, § 1; 468, § 1; 1178; 1330-1332; 1344; 2182-2185.

compelling the fulfillment of this duty.[29] Great emphasis was placed on the advantages of sacred missions so that pastors were urged to consider this obligation not as a burden but rather as an important help to them in the raising of the spiritual standards of their parishes.

There is no doubt that bishops could enact penalties in order to ensure that the diocesan regulations concerning the giving of sacred missions would be observed, but such measures would be taken only as a last resort after other measures had proved unsuccessful.[30]

[29] E.g., Ravenna (1865)—*Coll. Lac.*, VI, 187-195.

[30] Cann. 2220, § 1; 2221.

CHAPTER X

SPIRITUAL EXERCISES SIMILAR TO SACRED MISSIONS

Article 1. Exercises for Catholics

A. Lay Retreats

Sacred missions are intended for all the faithful in the parish, but naturally they are designed particularly for bringing sinners to repentance and the lax to a more fervent practice of their Catholic Faith. Evidently, however, there is need for spiritual exercises designed especially for those large numbers of the faithful who are striving after Christian perfection. The Church fills this need by encouraging retreats for the faithful as well as for the clergy.

St. Ignatius Loyola was the first to promote these retreats for the faithful on a large scale. His *Spiritual Exercises* were approved and encouraged by many popes.[1] Pope Pius VI defended these spiritual exercises along with sacred missions against the Synod of Pistoia (1786).[2] Particular councils and synods have also endorsed spiritual exercises or retreats for the laity.[3]

[1] E.g., Paulus III, litt. ap. *Pastoralis officii,* 31 iul. 1548; Alexander VII, litt. ap. *Cum sicut,* 12 oct. 1657; Benedictus XIV, litt. ap. *Quantum secessus,* 20 mart. 1753; littl. ap. *Dedimus sane,* 16 maii 1753 (these four documents are cited in Pope Pius XI's Encyclical Letter *Mens Nostra,* 20 dec. 1929—*AAS,* XXI [1929], 703-704); Leo XIII, ep. *Ignatianae commentationes,* 8 febr. 1900—*Leonis XIII Pontificis Maximi Acta* (23 vols., Romae, 1881-1905), VII, 373; Pius XI, const. *Summorum Pontificium,* 25 iul. 1922—*AAS,* XIV (1922), 42; litt. ap. *Meditantibus Nobis,* 3 dec. 1922—*AAS,* XIV (1922), 627; ep. encycl. *Mens Nostra,* 20 dec. 1929—*AAS,* XXI (1929), 689.

[2] Const. *Auctorem fidei,* 28 aug. 1794, ad LXV—*Fontes,* n. 475.

[3] E.g., Ponticherry (1844)—*Coll. Lac.,* VI, 660; Bordeaux (1850)—*op. cit.,* IV, 590; Tuam (1858)—*op. cit.,* III, 874-877; Strigonia (1858)—*op. cit.,* V, 76; Venice (1859)—*op. cit.,* VI, 317-318; Prague (1860)—*op. cit.,* V, 371; Calcoza (1863)—*op. cit.,* V, 713; Utrecht (1865)—*op. cit.,* V, 882; Baltimore II (1866)—*op. cit.,* III, 525-526; New Granada (1868)—*op. cit.,* VI, 540; *Acta et Decreta Concilii Plenarii Quebecensis I, anno 1909,* decr. 329;

The spiritual retreats or exercises given for the faithful in their parishes are often identified with sacred missions by legislation and by authors on the subject.[4] They differ, however, in their specific purpose. In a mission emphasis is placed upon the return to the sacraments and the adoption of a Christian mode of living. The sermon topics deal with the last things, perseverance, and the mercy of God, which topics are calculated to arouse the repentance of sinners. Frequent opportunities for confession are offered by two or more missioners. Retreats, on the other hand, are regularly given by one retreat master and emphasize the Christian virtues and the means for progressing in the spiritual life.[5]

Sometimes retreats are given for those who are preparing to receive their First Communion or the sacrament of confirmation, and they are also given for whole parishes in preparation for an important event in the ecclesiastical year, such as Easter.[6] Parochial retreats in the United States are seldom given, but regional or diocesan retreats for the laity are very common. Some dioceses have permanent retreat houses for the laity.[7] Many more dioceses have annual retreats for laymen and lay women.[8] Often, besides the general retreats for the laity, special retreats are given for various lay groups such as professional men and also for the laboring classes.[9] Particular legislation in the United States has also pointed out the value of retreats for the laity.[10] The Code definitely pre-

Concilium Plenarium Siculum, anno 1920, can. 22; *Concilium Plenarium Etruscum, anno 1933,* decr. 31, § 2 (These last two Italian councils are cited by McVann on page 155).

[4] E.g., Baltimore II (1866)—*Coll. Lac.,* III, 525-526, decree n. 473.

[5] McVann, p. 155.

[6] E.g., *Concilium Plenarium Siculum, anno 1920,* can. 20; *Concilium Plenarium Campanum, anno 1932,* decr. 44, §1; *Concilium Plenarium Etruscum, anno 1933,* decr. 31, § 2, (these councils are cited by McVann on page 155).

[7] E.g., New York, Boston, Philadelphia, Washington, Baltimore, Chicago.

[8] E.g., Atlanta, New Orleans, St. Louis, Portland in Oregon, Seattle, Helena.

[9] E.g., annual retreats for lawyers, doctors, policemen, and firemen in the Archdioceses of New York and Baltimore.

[10] ". . . Valde optandum est ut, quam citius fieri possit, secessus illi spirituales, quemadmodum pro clericis, et pro laicis instituantur ad normas ab Ordinario loci praescribendas, in quibus fideles per aliquot dies se colligere possint ad exercitia spiritualia peragenda . . ." *Acta et Decreta Concilii*

scribes retreats for members of the secular and religious clergy, either ordained or still in the seminary.[11] Retreats for the laity have been strongly recommended by the Holy See and by particular legislation but there is no obligation set.[12]

There now arises the question whether the holding of a parochial retreat would satisfy the decennial obligation of holding a sacred mission, as enacted in canon 1349. This particular point is not found in any legislation, nor is it treated by any of the authors on the subject. From what has already been seen about sacred missions it can safely be said that a parochial retreat would satisfy the obligation if it were held for the entire parish. It would not satisfy the obligation if it were held only for a particular group in the parish. The ideas of sacred missions and of parochial retreats have been so closely associated with each other in papal pronouncements and particular legislation that it is difficult at times to distinguish between them.[13]

Parochial retreats are governed by the same laws as missions. Outside retreat masters need the preaching faculty, which must be secured from the local ordinary, and the proper canonical procedure must be followed.[14] If a parochial retreat is to take the place of a sacred mission, it should afford the same frequent opportunities for confession, and it should be extended for at least a week, as is the general practice in a sacred mission. In order to satisfy the obligation of canon 1349, the parochial retreat must include the essential characteristics of the sacred mission.

Provincialis Portlandensis in Oregon IX, anno 1932, decr. 42; cf. also the following synods: *Constitutiones Dioeceseos Sinus Viridis Quartae Synodi Dioecesanae, anno 1920,* n. 281; *Code of the Diocese of Des Moines Decreed in Diocesan Synod on June 15, 1923,* n. 349; *Liber Synodalis Fargensis I, anno 1941,* stat. 528; *Synodus Dioecesana Toletana in America Prima, anno 1941,* n. 291.

11 Cann. 126; 541; 571, § 3; 595, § 1, 1°; 1001; 1367, § 4.

12 Wernz-Vidal, *Ius Canonicum,* Vol. IV, Pars. II, 67.

13 E.g., Pius VI, const. *Auctorem fidei,* 28 aug. 1794—*Fontes,* n. 475; Baltimore II (1866)—*Coll. Lac., III,* 466, 525-526, decrees n. 260 and n. 473.

14 McVann, p. 155; Wernz-Vidal, *Ius Canonicum,* Vol. IV, Pars. II, 68.

B. Days of Recollection

In late years one-day retreats or days of recollection have become popular, especially in the United States. They are held regularly by some parishes and by various lay groups.[15] These days of recollection have proved popular because many who are unable to attend a full retreat are still able to take advantage of these exercises.

Could a pastor, by holding a regular monthly day of recollection, satisfy the obligation enacted in canon 1349? Since the Code does not rule on how the mission is to be given, and since the Holy See has given no further directives, there seems at first sight to be nothing in the universal law that would be opposed to such a procedure. A closer examination of the words of the canon, however, will reveal that some indication is given concerning the intention of the legislator. Canon 1349, § 1, states that what is called a sacred mission should be held every ten years. It is necessary, then, that the conducted exercises be commonly recognized as being of the nature of a mission. It is easy to see how spiritual exercises in the form of retreats could satisfy the obligation, for they have been intimately connected with sacred missions in their history and in the pertinent legislation. On the other hand, monthly days of recollection undoubtedly fill a very great need, but they are lacking in some of the characteristic features of a sacred mission.

It is certain that the Holy See and the various particular councils and synods did not envisage separated monthly days of recollection when they spoke of spiritual exercises and missions. A sacred mission has always been regarded as a continuous series of spiritual exercises closely integrated and with a definite purpose in mind. Monthly days of recollection lack the continuity of a sacred mission, and would not be recognized as a mission.

For the same reason a pastor could not consider the conducted Advent or Lenten devotions in his parish as the equivalent of a sacred mission, and thus satisfy the obligation. Missions could indeed be held in Advent or Lent, and thus incidentally could take the place

[15] E.g., Holy Name Society, Knights of Columbus, Legion of Mary, Catholic Daughters of America, Third Orders, Catholic Action Groups, Cana Conferences, and numerous sodalities, confraternities, etc.

of the regular devotions. In fact, as has already been noted, the penitential seasons have been long recommended as appropriate times for sacred missions. Special *tridua* or novenas would not fulfill the obligation unless they correspond to the nature of a mission and are held for the same purpose.

The Forty Hours' Devotion at one time was closely connected with sacred missions, but this devotion alone would not satisfy the obligation. Even in the sixteenth century when the two were intimately related, the *Forty Hours' Devotion* served only as a solemn introduction or conclusion to the sacred mission.[16]

The *Forty Hours' Devotion* should be held every year, on days to be determined by the local ordinary, in all the parish churches and in the other churches in which the Blessed Sacrament is habitually reserved.[17] It is not proper, and it is certainly against the mind of the legislator, that the two obligations enacted in canons 1275 and 1349 be satisfied simultaneously. Furthermore, the essential characteristics of the *Forty Hours' Devotion,* so minutely portrayed and regulated in the *Clementine Instruction*[18], are not in accord with the traditional concept of a sacred mission. Despite the divergent common practice today, sermons are not called for at a *Forty Hours' Devotion.*[19] It is rather a time for adoration, and for recollection and silence. If anything is to be added to the ceremonies prescribed by the rubrics, oral prayers or a brief *ferverino* on the Holy Eucharist would be more in accord with the proper spirit of the *Forty Hours' Devotion.*

[16] Zawart, "History of Franciscan Preaching and Preachers" *Franciscan Educational Conference,* IX (1927), 391-393.

[17] Can. 1275.

[18] Clemens XI, *Instructio pro Expositione SS. Sacramenti in Forma XL Horarum,* 20 ian. 1705—*Decreta Authentica Congregationis Sacrorum Rituum ex actis eiusdem collecta eiusque auctoritate promulgata* (5 vols. et 2 appendices, Romae, 1898-1927), IV, 3-151 (hereafter cited *Decr. Auth. S. R. C.*).

[19] ". . . Nel tempo, che durerà l'Orazione medesima, si proibisce espressamente il predicare, ma volendo fare dopo li Vesperi qualche breve sermone per eccitare li fedeli alla devozione verso il SSmo Sagramento, si dovrà prendere la licenza e benedizione da Noi o da Monsignor nostro Vicegerente, anche nelle Chiese de' Regolari ed in qualunque modo privilegiate; e non solo nell' Esposizione di Quarant'ore, ma in qualsivoglia altra Esposizione; la quale licenza si darà in *scriptis* . . ."—*Decr. Auth. S. R. C.*, IV, 118.

ARTICLE 2. EXERCISES FOR NON-CATHOLICS

A. Non-Catholic Missions

Bishops and pastors are reminded by the Code that they are to look after the spiritual welfare of the non-Catholics as well as the faithful in their dioceses and parishes.[20] This instruction of the Code is based on the divine law.[21] It is evident, then, that a serious obligation is placed upon bishops and pastors to do what is in their power to bring about the conversion of non-Catholics. The local ordinaries as mentioned here do no include vicars or prefects apostolic, nor do the pastors include quasi-pastors. Canon 1350, § 2, makes all efforts for the conversion of non-Catholics in missionary territories subject to the special directions of the Sacred Congregation for the Propagation of the Faith.[22]

No definite procedure is outlined by the Holy See for the use of bishops and pastors in their apostolates for non-Catholics. Rather, the means are left to the prudent discretion of the local ordinaries. Some positive program for the conversion of non-Catholics is evidently called for, not merely the negative attitude of waiting for the non-Catholics to come and ask for instructions. This program should have three essential features on its *agenda:* prayer, distribution of literature and instruction where possible.[23]

One of the most effective means of procuring the conversion of non-Catholics has proved to be the mission for non-Catholics. Called mission, because it resembles in some respects the sacred mission for Catholics, this method has been successful largely through its emphasis on prayer and understanding rather than upon

[20] Can. 1350—§ 1. Ordinarii locorum et parochi acatholicos, in suis dioecesibus et paroeciis degentes, commendatos sibi in Domino habeant.

[21] Matt., XXVIII: 19, 20. Cf. Coronata, II, 275.

[22] "In aliis territoriis universa missionum cura apud acatholicos Sedi Apostolicae unice reservatur."

[23] Coronata, II, 275; Augustine, *A Commentary on the New Code of Canon Law* (2 ed., 8 vols., St. Louis: Herder, 1918-1924), VI, 370-371; Blat, *Commentarium Textus Codicis Iuris Canonici*, IV, 315; Cocchi, *Commentarium in Codicem Iuris Canonici*, VI, 67.

controversy. A non-Catholic mission generally consists of a series of lectures given in churches, halls, or even in the open.[24]

In late years the use of railroad chapel cars and automobile trailer chapels have enabled missionaries to contact Catholics and non-Catholice alike in the most remote districts. With the help of modern loud-speaking equipment, the missionaries are able to gather a crowd and present the truths of the Catholic Faith in comparatively easy fashion.[25]

Several religious communities have been particularly active in the non-Catholic missionary apostolate.[26] Diocesan apostolic mission bands, made up of the secular clergy, and established in many dioceses, have been engaged largely in conducting missions for non-Catholics.[27]

The approval by the Holy See of non-Catholic missions was given by Pope Leo XIII (1878-1903).[28] Particular legislation likewise has recommended the holding of missions for non-Catholics, though local ordinaries have at the same time invoked certain qualification in their conciliar enactments.[29] Ordinaries and pastors should take local conditions fully into account before embarking on a program of missions for non-Catholics. Sometimes it is necessary to prepare the way by the distribution of literature, so that the purpose of the mission for non-Catholics will be clearly understood. Special conditions may prevent public non-Catholic missions from

[24] McVann, p. 158-159.

[25] Cf. Klee, "Survey on Street Preaching," *The Priest* (Huntington, Ind., 1945—), I (1945), No. 8, 21-26, No. 9, 34-37; O'Brien, *Winning Converts, a Symposium on Methods of Convert Making for Priests and Lay People* (New York: P. J. Kenedy, 1948).

[26] E.g., the Passionists, the Redemptorists, and the Paulists.

[27] Doyle, "The Apostolic Missionary House," *The Catholic Church in the United States of America* (3 vols., New York: The Catholic Editing Co., 1912-1914), I, 459-467.

[28] Ep. *Testem benevolentiae*, 22 ian. 1899—*ASS*, XXXI (1899), 478-479; *Fontes*, n. 640.

[29] E.g., *Acta et Decreta Concilii Plenarii Quebecensis I, anno 1909*, n. 332; *Acta et Decreta Concilii Provincialis Portlandensis in Oregon, anno 1932*, decr. 39.

being advantageous, and it may be necessary to concentrate on individual instructions for non-Catholics.[30]

B. Inquiry Classes

Although it may often prove difficult or inopportune to hold missions for non-Catholics, inquiry classes, conducted on a parochial basis, have had nearly universal appeal. These classes are usually conducted by the pastor or his assistants in the individual parishes. The help of Catholic parishioners in bringing their non-Catholic spouses, relatives, and friends to the proposed inquiry class is solicited from the pulpit several Sundays before the opening of the class. A course in the fundamental doctrines of the Catholic Faith is given, usually in two hourly classes a week, covering a period of at least three months. At the end of that time the class is dismissed, and private instruction is arranged for prospective converts. The use of motion pictures and slides has in recent years been a development that has furnished a valuable aid in the giving of the lectures.

These inquiry classes have become very common, particularly in the United States, and their usefulness has been pointed out in particular legislation.[31] Pastors in many parishes hold a continuous inquiry class for all converts. Other pastors feel that converts should be given private instructions, and that inquiry classes should be held only as a last resort. This latter opinion concerning the superior advantages of private instruction undoubtedly has very strong points in its favor, and it could readily enough be reduced to practice in sections of the country where Catholics reside in large numbers, so that the number of converts would relatively remain

[30] Woywod, "On Preaching," *Hom. & Pas. Rev.*, XXVIII (1929), 176.

[31] ". . . *Sacerdotes nullum intermittant conamen, nulli parcant labori ut infideles et haeretici ad verae Fidei notitiam adducantur, argumentis adhibitis quae pro praesenti tempore et nostra regione urgentioris sint valoris. Hortamur parochos ut in suis paroeciis instituant quae vocantur* 'Inquiry Classes' . . ." —*Acta et Decreta Concilii Provincialis Portlandensis in Oregon, anno 1932,* decr. 40, § 1; *Synodus Dioecesana Richmondiensis Tertia, anno 1932,* stat. 124; *Synodus Dioecesana Seattlensis, anno 1938,* stat. 68; *Synodus Dioecesana Toletana in America Prima, anno 1941,* n. 292; *Liber Synodalis Fargensis I, anno 1941,* stat. 513; *The Ninth Synod of Harrisburg,* 1943, Appendix XI, n. 4.

quite small. In many sections, however, it would be impossible to hold private convert instructions in view of the large numbers who wish to take instructions and in consequence of the scarcity of priests who can wait upon them. The use of convert or inquiry classes has frequently proved to be the only practicable solution.

Even where Catholics are in the majority, some efforts should be made to attract non-Catholics to come for instruction, whether through inquiry classes or through other methods. Failure to make any attempt to contact non-Catholics, when no sufficiently grave reason warrants such a passive attitude, would amount to a disregard for the obligation stated in canon 1350, § 1.

In all convert work prudence and caution are absolutely necessary. Priests are forbidden to entice non-Catholics to join the Church if they are not fully ready for such a step.[32] Priests must exercise great care to see that converts have received a full instruction, lest they fall away from the Church in a short time.

Article 3. Exercises for Catholics and Non-Catholics

A. Conferences and Discussions

Although the Holy See has approved non-Catholic missions and inquiry classes, such approbation should not be construed as including inter-faith conferences or joint religious movements in which both Catholics and non-Catholics take part. Some conferences may be permitted, while others must be strictly forbidden. The differences between these two types of conferences are carefully distinguished by Kelleher:

> There are two fundamental types of conferences between religious bodies as such. One type is held for the specific and immediate purpose of bringing one or more non-Catholics into the true Church of Christ. Such a conference is of course good and laudable, yet before it can be entered into certain precautions must be taken lest there be any whittling down of dogmatic truths. In all other cases the religions involved preserve their peculiar identity before and after the conference. The mutual antagonism and rivalry are replaced by mutual collaboration and co-operation. With the recognition and acknowledgement of

[32] Can. 1351.

differences, the members of the various religious groups strive for one end by means of common or parallel action.

Conferences of this second type may be divided into three groups: (1) those which aim at a union of the churches with due allowance for particular differences; (2) those which strive for mutual tolerance without formal union, and (3) those which are concerned primarily with moral, social or civic issues.[33]

According to Kelleher and other authors, participation by Catholics in this second type of conferences will be governed by two fundamental principles of the Church. The first is the law of fraternal charity. Regardless of race, creed, or color, Catholics must love all men and be ready to assist them in any way that they can. Since the Catholic Church was founded by Christ for the salvation of all men, the first object of fraternal charity should be to bring those outside of the Church into the fold.

This first principle, however, must be regulated and controlled by the second, which is the fundamental doctrine that Catholicism is the only true religion and that Catholics may not give positive approval or assistance, in any way, to the propagation of a non-Catholic religion, for no religion but the Catholic religion has an objective right to exist in the light of the divine law.[34] The Catholic Church cannot allow, either by word or action, the impression that the various erroneous religious sects are to be treated as equals.

Admittedly, it is not an easy matter to reconcile these two principles when dealing with a practical case, but some conclusions can be drawn from them and from the attitude taken by the Holy See on the subject. Conferences whose aim is to reduce all religions to a common denominator are strictly forbidden. Likewise, conferences which respect the diverse religious beliefs of various sects and are intended to promote tolerance for the various beliefs are forbidden, for truth cannot be tolerant of error.

On the other hand, Catholics may be permitted to participate in conferences which are organized solely for moral, social, civil,

[33] *Discussions With Non-Catholics*, The Catholic University of America Canon Law Studies, n. 180 (Washington, D. C.: The Catholic University of America Press, 1943), pp. 46-47.

[34] Kelleher, *op. cit.*, p. 49.

or charitable purposes, provided that the danger of religious indifferentism is sufficiently guarded against. Such participation is often necessary in order to achieve the common good.

Great caution must be exercised by all Catholics should circumstances permit their participation in conferences with non-Catholics. Often enough the conferences which were organized for purely civic or charitable purposes soon become the occasion for the making of generalized statements on religion.

Catholics are often asked to join in observance of *brotherhood weeks, religious revival weeks, united prayer movements, and the* like. While ostensibly the beliefs and practices of all religions are respected by such undertakings, actually the attitude of religious indifferentism is cultivated. The apparent good of these inter-faith movements often deceives Catholics, who do not see any reason why they cannot co-operate with their non-Catholic brethren in forwarding what they believe to be the cause of all religion.

The possibility of bringing large groups of non-Catholics into the Church has often encouraged some Catholics to take part in inter-faith discussions. The Holy Office has repeatedly expressed its disapproval of such a practice.[35] Pope Pius XI confirmed the resolutions of the Holy Office on this subject.[36]

It is disputed whether the permission of the Holy See is necessary for participation in conferences and discussions with non-Catholics. Some authors hold that they fall within the scope of canon 1325, § 3.[37] Others declare that conferences and discussions are not included [38], for, as they maintain, only disputations and debates are mentioned in canon 1325, § 3.[39]

[35] Cf. *AAS*, XI (1919), 309-316; XIX (1927), 278.

[36] Ep. encycl. *Mortalium animos*, 10 ian. 1928—*AAS*, XX (1928), 5-16.

[37] Bouscaren, "Cooperation with Non-Catholics, Canonical Legislation," *Theological Studies* (Baltimore, 1940—), III (1942), 504; Connell, "Catholics and Interfaith Groups," *ER*, CV (1942), 342; McVann, p. 157.
Ordinarii."

[38] Kelleher, *op. cit.*, p. 71; Wernz-Vidal, *Ius Canonicum*, Vol. IV, Pars II, n. 619; Coronata, II, 912; Beste, *Introductio in Codicem*, p. 646.

[39] "Caveant catholici ne disputationes vel collationes, publicas praesertim, cum acatholicis habeant, sine venia Sanctae Sedis aut, si casus urgeat, loci Ordinarii."

According to this latter opinion, permission for conferences and discussions needs to be obtained not indeed from the Holy See, but rather from the local ordinary alone. This opinion appeared to be safe and sound for conferences and discussions did not appear to be explicitly mentioned in canon 1325, § 3. In the pre-Code law, *collationes* was used commonly as a synonym for *disputationes* and in virtue of canon 6, 4° the commentators maintain that only formal debates need the permission of the Holy See. Yet a recent monitum of the Holy See indicates the need of permission from the Holy See, in accordance with the norm of canon 1325, § 3, when there is question of taking part in mixed gatherings, wherein matters of the Faith are discussed between non-Catholics and Catholics.[40]

Evidently all mixed gatherings of Catholics and non-Catholics, if they deal with matters relating to the Faith, are to be governed by the rule which is stated in canon 1325, § 3. In view of this directive from the Holy Office, ordinaries should, unless there is urgency, obtain permission from the Holy See before it becomes allowable for Catholics to participate in conferences and discussions with non-Catholics in such mixed gatherings. Even though the required permission has been obtained from the Holy See, the conferences and discussions remain entirely under the control and supervision of the bishop, who in his diocese is the custodian of the matters that pertain to faith and morals.

[40] S. C. S. Off., Monitum, 5 iun. 1948:—Cum compertum sit variis in locis, contra Sacrorum Canonum praescripta et sine praevia S. Sedis venia, mixtos conventus acatholicorum cum catholicis habitos fuisse, in quibus de rebus fidei tractatum est, omnibus in memoriam revocatur ad normam canonis 1325, § 3, prohibitum esse quominus his conventibus intersint, sine praedicta venia, cum laici, tum clerici sive saeculares sive religiosi. Multo autem minus catholicis licitum est huiusmodi conventus convocare et instituere. Quapropter Ordinarii urgeant, ut haec praescripta ab omnibus adamussin serventur.

Quae quidem potiore iure observanda sunt, cum agitur de conventibus, quos 'oecumenicos' vocant, quibus catholici, sive laici sive clerici, sine S. Sedis praevio consensu, nullo modo interesse possunt.

Cum vero, tum in praedictis conventibus tum extra ipsos, etiam actus mixti cultus haud raro positi fuerint, denuo omnes monentur quamlibet in sacris communicationem ad normam canonum 1258 et 731, § 2, omnino prohibitam esse.—*AAS*, XL (1948), 257; *The Jurist* (Wash., D. C., 1941—), VIII (1948), 471.

In the past, bishops themselves have taken part in interfaith conferences. The Holy See has shown that it does not endorse such actions; it prefers a different approach, namely that of the non-Catholic mission or also that of the inquiry class for non-Catholics.[41]

B. Debates and Disputations

As has already been seen, debates and disputations with non-Catholics, whether public or private, clearly fall under the rule of canon 1325, § 3, and therefore require the permission of the Holy See. In an urgent case the local ordinary has the power to grant this permission. The canon refers, of course, only to debates and disputations which are concerned with matters of faith or of morals. Both private as well as public debates are thus proscribed, as long as they have been formally prepared beforehand. Permission for a private debate or disputation would more readily be given than for one of a public nature.[42]

In recent years, controversies between Christians on the one hand, and Communists and free-thinkers on the other, have become increasingly common. Catholics are prohibited from having part in such disputations unless the permission of the Holy See has been granted. The decrees of the Sacred Congregation for the Propagation of the Faith indicate that Catholics may not participate with non-Catholics in disputations, whether the non-Catholics are heretics, apostates, schismatics, Jews, or infidels.[43]

[41] Litt. ap. de coetibus vulgo dictis "Parliaments of Religion," 28 Sept., 1895 (to the apostolic delegate at Washington, D. C.)—*AER*, XIII (1895), 395.

[42] Kelleher, op. cit., p. 41; *The Jurist*, V (1945), 293.

[43] Kelleher, *op. cit.*, p. 36.

CONCLUSIONS

1. Sacred missions owe their remote origin to the popular preaching developed by the Mendicant Orders in the thirteenth century, and their proximate origin to the emphasis on preaching in the Counter-Reformation of the sixteenth century.

2. Contrary to popular belief, missions were not introduced by St. Vincent de Paul in 1627. The first missions, although not always called such, were given by the Jesuits and Capuchins in the latter part of the sixteenth and in the early part of the seventeenth centuries.

3. The development of missions by St. Vincent de Paul and his Congregation apparently was not influenced by the previous Jesuit and Capuchin missions.

4. The statement of St. Alphonsus Liguori, namely, that a good pastor has a sacred mission at least every four or five years, served as a norm for most of the legislation of the nineteenth and early twentieth centuries.

5. Although there was no universal pre-Code law which made the holding of sacred missions obligatory, the recommendations of the Holy See and of local authorities, in addition to the common practice, did not allow a pastor in good faith to forego completely the use of sacred missions in his parish.

6. During the thirty years which have elapsed since the enactment of the Code, the average interval as enacted in particular legislation for the holding of missions may be designated as five years.

7. Despite the opinion of some authors, e.g., of Blat, the ordinaries mentioned in canon 1349, § 1, are to be understood in the exclusive sense of local ordinaries, and not also in the sense of major religious superiors.

8. All particular legislation on sacred missions, if it has not subsequently been revoked, remains in force as long as it is not contrary to the obligation, as specified in the Code, of holding missions at least every ten years.

9. The provisions of the II Council of Baltimore (1866) on

sacred missions and missionaries are to be considered as strong recommendations rather than as obligations in law.

10. Both general and particular missions are allowed, but the holding of a single mission for the simultaneous participation of a number of parishes falls short of the obligation which calls for the holding of individual parish missions.

11. No specific penalties are enacted in the universal law or in particular legislation, as far as the writer could ascertain, for the failure to fulfill the obligation of holding sacred missions in parishes.

12. Parochial retreats satisfy the obligation of holding missions as long as they are held for all the parishioners and retain the essential characteristics of sacred missions.

13. The *Forty Hours' Devotion,* novenas, *tridua,* days of recollection and other such spiritual exercises are essentially different from sacred missions, and therefore cannot be utilized in fulfillment of the obligation of holding missions in the parishes.

14. Bishops and pastors are bound to use suitable means, e. g., non-Catholic missions or inquiry classes, for approaching the non-Catholics in their dioceses and parishes with the purpose of gaining their conversion to the Faith.

BIBLIOGRAPHY

Sources

Acta Apostolicae Sedis, Commentarium Officiale, Romae, 1909—

Acta et Decreta Concilii Plenarii Americae Latinae, anno 1899, Romae, 1902, appendix, 1906.

Acta et Decreta Concilii Plenarii Australiensis II, anno 1895, Sydney, 1898.

Acta et Decreta Concilii Plenarii Baltimorensis III, anno 1886, Baltimorae: Typis Ioannis Murphy et Sociorum, 1886.

Acta et Decreta Concilii Plenarii Episcoporum Hiberniae, habitae apud Maynutiam, anno 1927, Dublin: Browne et Nolan, 1929.

Acta et Decreta Concilii Plenarii Quebecensis I, anno 1909, Quebeci, 1912.

Acta et Decreta Concilii Provincialis Mechliniensis IV, anno 1920, Mechliniae: H. Dessain, 1923.

Acta et Decreta Concilii Provincialis Portlandensis in Oregon IV, anno 1932, Portland, Ore., 1934.

Acta et Decreta Concilii Provincialis Tuamensis, anno 1933, Galviae: O'Gorman, 1935.

Acta et Decreta Sacrorum Conciliorum Recentium, Collectio Lacensis, 7 vols., Friburgi Brisgoviae: Herder, 1870-1892.

Acta et Decreta Synodi Dioecesanae Quebecensis Secundae, anno 1940, Quebeci, 1940.

Acta et Decreta Synodi Dioecesanae Toletanae in America Primae, anno 1943, Toledo, Ohio, 1943.

Acta et Decreta Synodi Plenariae Episcoporum Hiberniae, habitae apud Maynutiam, anno 1875, Dublin: Browne et Nolan, 1877.

Acta et Statuta Synodi Richmondiensis Secundae, anno 1886, Richmond, 1886.

Acta Sanctae Sedis, 41 vols., Romae, 1865-1908.

Analecta Ecclesiastica, 18 vols., Romae, 1893-1911.

Bullarii Romani Continuatio, edita ab A. Barberi, A. Spetia et R. Segreti, 20 vols., Romae, 1835-1857.

Bullarium Benedicti XIV, 4 vols., Romae: Typis Sacrae Congregationis de Propaganda Fide, 1746-1763.

Bullarum Diplomatum et Privilegiorum Sanctorum Romanorum Pontificum Taurinensis Editio, 24 vols. et Appendix, Augustae Taurinorum, 1857-1872.

Code of the Diocese of Des Moines Decreed in the First Diocesan Synod, June 15, 1923, Des Moines, 1923.

Codex Iuris Canonici Pii X Pontificis Maximi iussu digestus Benedicti Papae XV auctoritate promulgatus, Romae: Typis Polyglottis Vaticanis, 1917.

Codicis Iuris Canonici Fontes, cura Emi Petri Card. Gasparri editi, 9 vols., Romae (postea Civitate Vaticana): Typis Polyglottis Vaticanis, 1923-1939. (Vols. VII-IX ed. cura et studio Emi Iustiniani Card. Serédi.)

Collectanea in Usum Secretariae Sacrae Congregationis Episcoporum et Regularium, ed. Bizzarri, Romae: Typographia Polyglotta S. C. de Propaganda Fide, 1885.

Collectanea Sacrae Congregationis de Propaganda Fide, Romae: Typographia Polyglotta S. C. de Propaganda Fide, 1893.

Constitutiones Dioecesanae Brooklyniensis Tertiae Synodi, anno 1894, Brooklyn, 1894.

Constitutiones Dioecesanae Carolopolitanae Synodi Dioecesanae Septimae Decimae, anno 1925, Charleston, 1925.

Constitutiones Dioecesanae II Synodi Dioecesis Bostoniensis, anno 1868, Boston, 1868.

Constitutiones Dioeceseos Bostoniensis Synodo Dioecesana Sexta, anno 1919, Boston, 1919.

Constitutiones Dioeceseos Natchensis, I Synodus, anno 1922 Natchez, 1922.

Constitutiones Dioeceseos Sinus Viridis Quartae Synodi Dioecesanae, anno 1928, Pulaski, Mich.: Typis Franciscanae Typographia, 1921.

Constitutiones Presbyterorum Societatis Mariae, Augustae Taurinorum: Schola Typographia Salesiana, 1923.

Constitutions of the Diocese of Lafayette, La., The Third Synod, 1943, Lafayette, La., 1943.

Corpus Iuris Canonici, Editio Lipsiensis II, Richter-Friedberg, 2 vols., Lipsieae, 1879-1881, editio anastatice repetita, Lipsiae: Tauchnitz, 1922.

Decreta Authentica Congregationis Sacrorum Rituum ex actis eiusdem collecta eiusque auctoritate promulgata, 5 vols. et 2 Appendices, Romae, 1898-1927.

Decreta Synodi Dioecesanae Mobiliensis Tertiae, anno 1921, Mobile, 1921.

Dioecesana Prima Syracusiensis Synodus, anno 1887, Syracuse, 1887.

Dioecesana Synodus Alexandriae Prima, anno 1923, Alexandria, La., 1923.

Dioecesana Synodus Petriculana Prima, anno 1909, Little Rock, 1909.

Dioecesana Synodus Sancti Ludovici Septima, anno 1929, St. Louis, 1929.

Estatutos Sinodales de la Diocesis de San Cristobal, Venuezuela, 1936, Typographia Diocesana, 1936.

First Synod of the Diocese of Owensboro, The, 1943, Owensboro, 1943.

Hardouin, Ioannes, *Acta Conciliorum et Epistolae Decretales ac Constitutiones Summorum Pontificum*, 12 vols., Parisiis, 1714-1715.

Labbeus, Philippus, et Cossartius, Gabriel, *Sacrosancta Concilia ad Regiam Editionem Exacta*, 17 vols., Lutetiae Parisiorum, 1671-1672.

Leonis XIII Pontificis Maximi Acta, 23 vols., Romae, 1881-1905.

Liber Synodalis Dioecesis Fargensis I, anno 1941, Milwaukee: Bruce, 1941.

Mansi, Ioannes, *Sacrorum Conciliorum Nova et Amplissima Collectio*, 53 vols. in 60, Parisiis, Arnhem et Leipzig, 1901-1927.

Ninth Synod of Harrisburg, The, 1943, Harrisburg, 1943.

Primum Concilium Sinense, anno 1924, Zi-Ka-Wei: Typographia Missionis Catholicae, 1929.

Schroeder, H. J., *Canons and Decrees of the Council of Trent*, St. Louis: B. Herder, 1941.

Sinodo Diocesano del Obispado de Puerto Rico, 1917, Puerto Rico, 1917.

Statuta Archidioecesanae Synodi Secundae Sancti Francisci, anno 1936, San Francisco, 1936.

Statuta Dioecesanae Angelorum et Sancti Didaci Lata ac Promulgata in Synodo Quinta, anno 1927, St. Louis: Herder, 1927.

Statuta Dioecesanae Synodi Quartae Leavenworthensis, anno 1922, Leavenworth, 1922 (since 1947, Kansas City in Kansas).

Statuta Dioecesanae Synodi Spokanensis Primae, anno 1939, Spokane, 1939.

Statuta Dioecesis Bellevillensis V Synodus, anno 1939, Belleville, 1939.

Statuta Dioecesis Lacus Salsi Lata ac Promulgata in Synodo Dioecesana Prima, anno 1929, Salt Lake City, 1929.

Statuta Dioecesis Montereyensis-Fresnensis in Prima Synodo Dioecesana Lata ac Promulgata, anno 1929, Monterey-Fresno, 1929.

Statuta Dioecesis Ogdensburgensis XIII Synodi, anno 1926, Ogdensburg 1926.

Statuta Dioecesis Pittsburgensis IV Synodi, anno 1920, Pittsburgh, 1920.

Statuta Dioecesis Savannensis-Atlantensis, I Synodus, anno 1939, Atlanta, 1939.

Statuta Dioecesis Seattlensis Lata ac Promulgata in Synodo Dioecesana Quinta, anno 1938, Seattle: Typis Metropolitanis, 1938.

Statuta Synodalia Dioecesis Argentinensis, anno 1923, Argentorati: Typis Francisci Xaverii Le Roux, 1923.

Statutes of the Diocese of Crookston Promulgated at the First Diocesan Synod held September 20, 1921, St. Louis: Herder, 1923.

Statutes of the Diocese of Lincoln Promulgated at the First Diocesan Synod, 1934, Lincoln, 1934.

Statutes of the Diocese of Pueblo, First Diocesan Synod, 1948, Pueblo, 1948.

Statutes of the Diocese of Wheeling Promulgated at the First Diocesan Synod, 1923, Wheeling, 1923.

Synodus I Altunensis, anno 1922, Altoona, 1922.

Synodus Archidioeceseos Indianapolitanae (I) Septima, anno 1947, Indianapolis, 1947.

Synodus Archidioecesana Portlandensis in Oregon, anno 1935, Portland, Ore., 1935.

Synodus Dioecesana Brooklyniensis Quinta, anno 1926, Brooklyn, 1926.

Synodus Dioecesana Buffalensis Vigesima Septima, anno 1924, Buffalo, 1924.

Synodus Dioecesana Cajetana Sexta, anno 1934, M. D'Auria & Sedis Apostolicae Typographus, Neapoli, 1935.

Synodus Dioecesana Cincinnatensis Quarta, anno 1920, Cincinnati, 1920.

Synodus Dioecesana Dallasensis Secunda, anno 1927, Dallas, 1927.

Synodus Dioecesana Denveriensis Quarta, anno 1904, Denver, 1904.

Synodus Dioecesana Elpasensis Prima, anno 1930, El Paso, 1930.

Synodus Dioecesana Greatormensis Prima, anno 1935, Great Falls, 1935.

Synodus Dioecesana Ogdensburgensis Prima, anno 1886, Ogdensburg, 1886.

Synodus Dioecesana Omahensis Quarta, anno 1934, Omaha, 1934.

Synodus Dioecesana Neo-Eboracensis Quinta, anno 1886, New York, 1886.

Synodus Dioecesana Richmondiensis Tertia, anno 1932, Richmond, 1932.

Synodus Dioecesana Rockfordensis Prima, anno 1916, Mayer et Miller: Chicageni, 1916.
Synodus Dioecesana Sancti Ludovici Septima, anno 1929, St. Louis: Herder, 1929.
Synodus Dioecesana Syracusensis Undecima, anno 1921, Syracuse, 1921.
Synodus Dioecesana Trentonensis Tertia, anno 1936, Trenton, 1936.
Synodus Dioecesana Wayne Castrensis, anno 1927, Fort Wayne, 1927.
Synodus Dioecesana Xylopolitana Secunda, anno 1941, Boise, 1941.
Synodus Dioecesis Albanensis Tertia, anno 1884, Albany, 1884.
Synodus Dioecesis Buffalensis Vigesima, anno 1886, Buffalo, 1886.
Synodus Grandormensis I, anno 1903, Grand Rapids, 1903.
Synodus Novae Aureliae Sexta, anno 1922, New Orleans, 1922.
Synodus Prima Manchesteriensis, anno 1886, Manchester, 1886.
Synodus Roffensis Tertia, anno 1914, Rochester, 1914.
Synodus Roffensis Quinta, anno 1935, Rochester, 1935.
Synodus Trentonensis II, anno 1897, Trenton, 1897.
Third Synod of Davenport, The, 1932, Davenport, 1932.

Reference Works

Aertnys, Iosephus, *Theologia Pastoralis,* Paderbornae, 1901.
Alphonsus M. de Liguori, St., *Homo Apostolicus,* Augustae Taurinorum: Marietti, 1876.
———, *The Complete Ascetical Works of Saint Alphonsus de Liguori,* Centenary Edition, 24 vols., New York: Benziger Bros., 1887-1893.
———, *Theologia Moralis,* ed. L. Gaudé, 4 vols., Romae, 1905-1912.
Augustine, Charles, *A Commentary on the New Code of Canon Law,* 2. ed., 8 vols., St. Louis, Mo.: B. Herder Book Co., 1918-1924. Vol. IV, 1921; Vol. VI, 1923; Vol. VIII, 1924.
Ayrinhac, H. A., *Administrative Legislation in the New Code of Canon Law,* New York: Longmans, Green and Co., 1930.
Bach, J. (ed.), *Histoire de S. François de Geronimo,* Metz, 1851.
Batiffol, P. H., *Primitive Catholicism,* translated by H. L. Brianceau, New York: Longmans, Green and Co., 1911.
Baudrillart, H., *The Catholic Church, the Renaissance and Protestantism,* translated by Mrs. Philip Gibbs, New York: Benziger Bros., 1908.
Berutti, Christophorus, *Institutiones Iuris Canonici,* Vol. IV, Taurini-Romae: Ex Officina Libraria Marietti, 1940.
Bergamaschi, F., *Dell' Origine delle SS. Quarantore,* Cremona, 1897.
Berthé, Augustine, *Saint Alphonse de Liguori,* 2 vols., Paris, 1907.
Beste, Uldericus, *Introductio in Codicem,* 3. ed., Collegeville, Minn.: St. John's Abbey Press, 1946.
Blat, Albertus, *Commentarium Textus Codicis Iuris Canonici,* Vol. IV, Romae: ex Typographia Pontificia in Instituto Pii IX, 1927.

Bondini, A., *De Privilegio Exemptionis seu de Regularium Immunitate ab Ordinariorum Locorum Iurisdictione prout in Novo Iuris Canonici Codice Sancitur,* Romae, 1919.

Catholic Church in the United States of America, The, 3 vols., New York: The Catholic Editing Co., 1912-1914.

Cavanaugh, J. W., *The Priests of the Holy Cross,* Notre Dame, Ind., 1905.

Cicognani, Amleto, *Canon Law,* translated by Joseph O'Hara and Francis Brennan, 2. rev. ed., Westminster, Md.: Newman, 1946.

Claeys-Bouuaert, F., et Simenon, G., *Manuale Juris Canonici,* 3 vols., Vol. II, 1931; Vols. I et III, 3. ed., Gandae et Leadii: in Seminariis Gandanensi et Leadiensi.

Cocchi, Guido, *Commentarium in Codicem Iuris Canonici ad Usum Scholarum,* Vol. VI, 3. ed., Taurinorum Augustae: ex Officina Libraria Marietti, 1933.

Coronata, Matthaeus Conte A., *Institutiones Iuris Canonici,* 2. ed., 5 vols., Romae: Marietti, 1939-1947.

Coste, Pierre, *Monsieur Vincent, le grand saint du grand siècle,* 3 vols., Paris: Desclée, 1931.

Currier, Charles W., *History of Religious Orders,* New York: Murphy & McCarthy, 1897.

Cuthbert (Hess), *The Capuchins,* 3 vols., New York: Longmans, Green and Co., 1929.

Dargan, Edwin C., *A History of Preaching,* New York: A. C. Armstrong & Son, 1905.

Daubenton, Guillaume, *La Vie du B. François Regis,* Paris, 1716.

De la Gorce, Pierre, *Histoire religieuse de la Revolution Francaise,* Paris, 1911.

De Montzey, M. C., *Father Eudes, Apostolic Missionary and His Foundations,* Boston: Patrick Donohoe, 1874.

Di Ormea, Salvatore, *Vita del B. Leonardo da Porto Maurizio,* Romae, 1851.

Donnelly, Francis B., *The Diocesan Synod,* The Catholic University of America Canon Law Studies, n. 74, Washington, D. C.: The Catholic University of America, 1932.

Eagleton, George, *The Diocesan Quinquennial Faculties Formula IV,* The Catholic University of America Canon Law Studies, n. 248, Washington, D. C.: The Catholic University of America Press, 1948.

Ferraris, Lucius, *Prompta Bibliotheca Canonica, Iuridica, Moralis, Theologica, nec non Ascetica, Polemica, Rubricistica, Historica,* 8 vols., Romae, 1885-1892; Bucceroni, Ianuarius, *Supplementum,* Romae, 1899.

Francis of Toulouse, *Le Missionaire Parfait,* 2 vols., Paris, 1662.

Hedley, John C., *Lex Levitarum,* London: Westminster Book Co., 1905.

Hinschius, P., *System des katholischen Kirchenrechts,* 4 vols., Berlin: Guttentag, 1869-1888.

Kassiepe, M., *Die katholische Volksmission in der neuen Zeit. Grundsätzliches und Praktisches für Seelsorger,* Paderborn: Verlag Ferdinand Schoningh, 1934.

Keene, Michael J., *Religious Ordinaries and Canon 198,* The Catholic University of America Canon Law Studies, n. 135, Washington, D. C.: The Catholic University of America Press, 1942.

Kelleher, Stephen J., *Discussions With Non-Catholics,* The Catholic University of America Canon Law Studies, n. 180, Washington, D. C.: The Catholic University of America Press, 1943.

McHugh, J. and Callan, C., *Catechism of the Council of Trent,* New York: Wagner, 1923.

Migne, Jacques P., *Patrologiae Cursus Completus, Series Latina,* 221 vols., Parisiis, 1844-1864.

Mourret, Ferdinand, and Thompson, Newton, *History of the Catholic Church,* 6 vols., St. Louis: Herder, 1930-1945.

Murphy, Francis J., *Legislative Powers of the Provincial Council,* The Catholic University of America Canon Law Studies, n. 257, Washington, D. C.: The Catholic University of America Press, 1947.

New Catholic Dictionary, The, New York: The Universal Knowledge Foundation, 1929.

New International Dictionary, Webster, 2. unabridg. ed., Springfield, Mass.: G. & C. Merriam, 1941.

New Testament of Our Lord and Saviour Jesus Christ, The, Revision of the Challoner-Rheims version by the Confraternity of Christian Doctrine, Paterson, N. J., St. Anthony's Guild, 1941.

Oakeley, Frederick, *The Priest on the Mission, a Course of Lectures on Missionary and Parochial Duties,* London: Longmans, Green and Co., 1871.

O'Brien, John, *Winning Converts, A Symposium on Methods of Convert Making for Priests and Lay People,* New York: P. J. Kenedy, 1948.

Ortolan, R. T., *Les Oblats de Marie Immaculée,* 2 vols., Paris, 1915.

Ottaviani, Alaphridus, *Compendium Iuris Publici Ecclesiastici,* Romae: Typis Polyglottis Vaticanis, 1936.

Pauvert, M., *Vie du venerable Louis Marie Grignion de Montfort,* Paris et Potiers, 1875.

Renninger, Johann, *Pastoral-Theologie,* Freiburg im Br.: Herder, 1893.

Ridley, Francis A., *The Jesuits, a Study in Counter-Reformation,* London: Secker & Warburg, 1938.

Robinson, George W., *Life of Saint Boniface by Willibald,* Cambridge, Mass.: Harvard University, 1917.

Rocco da Cesinale, *Storia delle Missioni dei Cappuccini,* 3 vols., Roma: Typografia Barbera, 1867-1873.

Saint Vincent de Paul, Correspondence, Entretiens, Documents, 40 vols. in 14, Paris, 1920-1925.

Schmidlin, J., *Catholic Mission History,* translated by Matthias Braun, Techny, Ill.: Mission Press, 1927.

———, *Catholic Mission Theory,* translated by Matthias Braun, Techny, Ill.: Mission Press, 1931.

Sebastianelli, Gulielmus, *Praelectiones Iuris Canonici*, 3 vols., Vol. I, *De Personis*, 2. ed. emendata et aucta, Romae: Pustet, 1905.

Slafkosky, Andrew L., *The Canonical Episcopal Visitation of the Diocese*, The Catholic University of America Canon Law Studies, n. 142, Washington, D. C.: The Catholic University of America Press, 1941.

Stebbing, George, *The Redemptorists*, New York: Benziger Bros., 1924.

Strayer, Joseph and Munro, Dana, *The Middle Ages*, The Century Historical Series, New York: D. Appleton-Century Co., 1928.

Thomassinus, L., *Vetus et Nova Disciplina circa Beneficia et Beneficarios*, Lugduni, 1706.

Vermeersch, Arturus, et Creusen, Iosephus, *Epitome Iuris Canonici*, 6. ed., 3 vols., Mechliniae et Romae: H. Dessain, 1937-1946.

Ward, Felix F., *Passionists: Sketches Historical and Personal*, New York: Benziger Bros., 1923.

Wernz, Franciscus X., *Ius Decretalium*, 6 vols., 2. ed., Romae: Prati, 1906-1913.

———, Vidal, Petrus, *Ius Canonicum ad Codicis Normam Exactum*, 7 tomes in 8 vols., Romae: apud aedes Universitatis Gregorianae, 1923-1938.

Wetenkampf, George, *Catholic Missions in the Early Middle Ages*, New York: Society for the Propagation of the Faith, 1944.

PERIODICALS

American Ecclesiastical Review, The, Philadelphia, 1889-1943 (published as *The Ecclesiastical Review*, July, 1905-December, 1943); Washington, D. C., 1944—

Archiv für katholiches Kirchenrecht, Innsbruck, 1857-1861; Mainz, 1862—

Commentarium pro Religiosis, Romae, 1920-1934; *Commentarium pro Religiosis et Missionariis*, 1935—

Franciscan Educational Conference, The, published annually, Brookland, Washington, D. C.: Capuchin College, 1919—

Homiletic and Pastoral Review, The, New York, 1900—

Il Monitore Ecclesiastico, Roma, 1876—

Il Pensitore Missione, Roma, 1929—

Jurist, The, Washington, D. C., 1941—

Le Canoniste Contemporain, Paris, 1878-1922; *Le Canoniste*, 1924-1926.

Priest, The, Huntington, Ind., 1945—

Sal Terrae, Santander, 1912—

Theological Studies, Baltimore, 1940—

Theologisch-praktische Quartalschrift, Linz, 1848—

ARTICLES

Bemelmans, J. H., "Missionaries of the Company of Mary," *The Catholic Encyclopedia*, IX, 749-750.

Bihl, M., "Leonard of Port Maurice," *The Catholic Encyclopedia*, IX, 178-179.

Bogsrücker, A., "Über Volkmissionen und Seelsorgaushilfen," *Theologisch-Quartalschrift*, LXXXV (1932), 370-375.

Bouscaren, T. L., "Cooperation With Non-Catholics, Canonical Legislation," *Theological Studies*, III (1942), 504.

"California Missions," *The New Catholic Dictionary*, p. 637.

Connell, Francis, "Catholics and Interfaith Groups," *Ecclesiastical Review*, CV (1942), 342.

Couly, J., "Des Missions," *Le Canoniste*, XLVI (1924), 288-293.

Doyle, J., "The Apostolic Missionary House," *The Catholic Church in the United States of America*, I, 459-467.

Gonzalez, M., "Los misiones parroquiales," *Sal Terrae*, IX (1920), 35-43, 120-132.

Healy, J., "Need of Parochial Missions," *The Homiletic and Pastoral Review*, XXI (1920), 177-181.

Hennrich, Kilian, "Concerning Parish Missions," *The Homiletic and Pastoral Review*, XLIII (1942), 182-183.

Henze, C. M., "De nova missionum paroecialium forma," *Commentarium pro Religiosis*, XV (1934), 56-64.

Kapistran, J., "Die Bedeutung der ausserordentlichen Seelsorge für die Pfarrei," *Theologisch-Praktische Quartalschrift*, LXXXI (1928), 37-50.

Klee, R., "Survey on Street Preaching," *The Priest*, I (1945), No. 7, 21-26, No. 8, 34-37.

Krull, V., "Parochial Missions," *The Ecclesiastical Review*, LXLV (1921), 614-616.

Maes, C. P., "Charles-Auguste-Marie-Joseph Comte de Forbin-Janson," *The Catholic Encyclopedia*, VI, 133-144.

Maroto, P., "Il dritto canonico e le missioni," *Il Pensitore Missione*, I (1929), 20-26.

Mills, F., "Preaching, the *Opus Franciscanum*," *The Franciscan Educational Conference*, IX (1927), 107-165.

Mueller, U. F., "Congregation of the Most Precious Blood," *The Catholic Encyclopedia*, XII, 373-375.

Pollen, J. H., "Counter-Reformation," *The Catholic Encyclopedia*, IV, 441-445.

Randolph, B., "Congregation of Priests of the Mission," *The Catholic Encyclopedia*, X, 359-368.

Schroeder, Joseph, "Mission, Catholic Parochial," *The Catholic Encyclopedia*, X, 391-394.

Woywod, S., "On Preaching," *The Homiletic and Pastoral Review*, XXVIII (1929), 178.

Zawart, Anscar, "History of Franciscan Preaching and Preachers," *The Franciscan Educational Conference*, IX (1927), 380-425.

ABBREVIATIONS

AAS—*Acta Apostolicae Sedis.*
AER—*The American Ecclesiastical Review.*
AKKR—*Archiv für katholisches Kirchenrecht.*
ASS—*Acta Sanctae Sedis.*
Bull. Benedicti XIV—*Bullarium Benedicti XIV.*
Bull. Rom. Taur.—*Bullarium Romanum, ed. Tauriensis.*
Bull. Rom. Cont.—*Bullarii Romani Continuatio.*
CE—*The Catholic Encyclopedia.*
Coll. Lac.—*Collectio Lacensis.*
Decr. Auth. S. R. C.—*Decreta Authentica Sacrorum Rituum Congreg.*
ER—*The Ecclesiastical Review.*
Fontes—*Codicis Iuris Canonici Fontes,* cura . . . Gasparri editi.
Hardouin—*Acta Conciliorum,* etc.
Hom. & Pas. Rev.—*The Homiletic and Pastoral Review.*
Labbeus-Cossartius—*Sacrosancta Concilia.*
Mansi—*Sacrorum Conciliorum Nova et Amplissima Collectio.*
MPL—Migne, *Patrologia Latina.*
S. C. Ep. et Reg.—Sacra Congregatio Episcoporum et Regularium.
S. C. de Prop. Fide—Sacra Congregatio de Propaganda Fide.
ThPrQs—*Theologisch-praktische Quartalschrift.*

ALPHABETICAL INDEX

BIOGRAPHICAL NOTE

Howard David Lavelle was born in Salt Lake City, Utah, on February 12, 1921. He received his elementary education at St. James Cathedral School, Seattle, Washington, and he attended O'Dea High School in Seattle, from which he graduated in June, 1938. In September, 1938, he entered St. Edward's Seminary, Kenmore, Washington, where he received the Bachelor of Arts Degree in June, 1942, and from which he was ordained priest on May 31, 1945. After one year of parochial work in the Diocese of Seattle, he enrolled, in September, 1946, in the School of Canon Law at The Catholic University of America, Washington, D. C., where he completed work for the Baccalaureate Degree in Canon Law in 1947, and for the Licentiate Degree in Canon Law in 1948.

CANON LAW STUDIES *

1. Freriks, Rev. Celestine A., C.PP.S., J.C.D., Religious Congregations in Their External Relations, 121 pp., 1916.
2. Gallíher, Rev. Daniel M., O.P., J.C.D., Canonical Elections, 117 pp., 1917.
3. Borkowski, Rev. Aurelius L., O.F.M., J.C.D., De Confraternitatibus Ecclesiasticis, 136 pp., 1918.
4. Castillo, Rev. Cayo, J.C.D., Disertacion Historico-Canonica sobre la Potestad del Cabildo en Sede Vacante o Impedida del Vicario Capitular, 99 pp., 1919 (1918).
5. Kubelbeck, Rev. William J., S.T.B., J.C.D., The Sacred Penitentiaria and Its Relation to Faculties of Ordinaries and Priests, 129 pp., 1918.
6. Petrovits, Rev. Joseph, J.C., S.T.D., J.C.D., The New Church Law on Matrimony, X-461 pp., 1919.
7. Hickey, Rev. John J., S.T.B., J.C.D., Irregularities and Simple Impediments in the New Code of Canon Law, 100 pp., 1920.
8. Klekotka, Rev. Peter J., S.T.B., J.C.D., Diocesan Consultors, 179 pp., 1920.
9. Wanenmacher, Rev. Francis, J.C.D., The Evidence in Ecclesiastical Procedure Affecting the Marriage Bond, 1920 (Printed 1935).
10. Golden, Rev. Henry Francis, J.C.D., Parochial Benefices in the New Code, IV-119 pp., 1921 (Printed 1925).
11. Koudelka, Rev. Charles J., J.C.D., Pastors, Their Rights and Duties According to the New Code of Canon Law, 211 pp., 1921.
12. Melo, Rev. Antonius, O.F.M., J.C.D., De Exemptione Regularium, X-188 pp., 1921.
13. Schaaf, Rev. Valentine Theodore, O.F.M., S.T.B., J.C.D., The Cloister, X-180 pp., 1921.
14. Burke, Rev. Thomas Joseph, S.T.D., J.C.D., Competence in Ecclesiastical Tribunals, IV-117 pp., 1922.
15. Leech, Rev. George Leo, J.C.D., A Comparative Study of the Constitution "Apostolicae Sedis" and the "Codex Juris Canonici," 179 pp., 1922.
16. Motry, Rev. Hubert Louis, S.T.D., J.C.D., Diocesan Faculties According to the Code of Canon Law, II-167 pp., 1922.
17. Murphy, Rev. George Lawrence, J.C.D., Delinquencies and Penalties in the Administration and the Reception of the Sacraments, IV-121 pp., 1923.
18. O'Reilly, Rev. John Anthony, S.T.B., J.C.D., Ecclesiastical Sepulture in the New Code of Canon Law, II-129 pp., 1923.

* All published numbers are available from the Catholic University of America Press, 620 Michigan Avenue, N.E., Washington 17, D. C., except the following: Nos. 1-114 inclusive, 116, 118, 120, 121, 122, 123, 136, 153, 162, 182 and 198. But the following numbers, now reissued, are obtainable from *The Jurist*, The Catholic University of America, Washington 17, D. C., namely: Nos. 5, 7, 11, 17, 18, 19, 26, 28, 30, 31, 34, 42, 44, 51, 52 and 61.

19. Michalicka, Rev. Wenceslas Cyrill, O.S.B., J.C.D., Judicial Procedure in Dismissal of Clerical Exempt Religious, 107 pp., 1923.
20. Dargin, Rev. Edward Vincent, S.T.B., J.C.D., Reserved Cases According to the Code of Canon Law, IV-103 pp., 1924.
21. Godfrey, Rev. John A., S.T.B., J.C.D., The Right of Patronage According to the Code of Canon Law, 153 pp., 1924.
22. Hagedorn, Rev. Francis Edward, J.C.D., General Legislation on Indulgences, II-154 pp., 1924.
23. King, Rev. James Ignatius, J.C.D., The Administration of the Sacraments to Dying Non-Catholics, V-141 pp., 1924.
24. Winslow, Rev. Francis Joseph, O.F.M., J.C.D., Vicars and Prefects Apostolic, IV-149 pp., 1924.
25. Correa, Rev. Jose Servelion, S.T.L., J.C.D., La Potestad Legislativa de la Iglesia Catolica, IV-127 pp., 1925.
26. Dugan, Rev. Henry Francis, A.M., J.C.D., The Judiciary Department of the Diocesan Curia, 87 pp., 1925.
27. Keller, Rev. Charles Frederick, S.T.B., J.C.D., Mass Stipends, 167 pp., 1925.
28. Paschang, Rev. John Linus, J.C.D., The Sacramentals According to the Code of Canon Law, 129 pp., 1925.
29. Piontek, Rev. Cyrillus, O.F.M., S.T.B., J.C.D., De Indulto Exclaustrationis necnon Saecularizationis, XIII-289 pp., 1925.
30. Kearney, Rev. Richard Joseph, S.T.B., J.C.D., Sponsors at Baptism According to the Code of Canon Law, IV-127 pp., 1925.
31. Bartlett, Rev. Chester Joseph, A.M., LL.B., J.C.D., The Tenure of Parochial Property in the United States of America, V-108 pp., 1926.
32. Kilker, Rev. Adrian Jerome, J.C.D., Extreme Unction, V-425 pp., 1926.
33. McCormick, Rev. Robert Emmett, J.C.D., Confessors of Religious, VIII-266 pp., 1926.
34. Miller, Rev. Newton Thomas, J.C.D., Founded Masses According to the Code of Canon Law, VII-93 pp., 1926.
35. Roelker, Rev. Edward G., S.T.D., J.C.D., Principles of Privilege According to the Code of Canon Law, XI-166 pp., 1926.
36. Bakalarczyk, Rev. Richardus, M.I.C., J.U.D., De Novitiatu, VIII-208 pp., 1927.
37. Pizzuti, Rev. Lawrence, O.F.M., J.U.L., De Parochis Religiosis, 1927. (Not Printed.)
38. Bliley, Rev. Nicholas Martin, O.S.B., J.C.D., Altars According to the Code of Canon Law, XIX-132 pp., 1927.
39. Brown, Mr. Brendan Francis, A.B., LL.M., J.U.D., The Canonical Juristic Personality with Special Reference to Its Status in the United States of America, V-212 pp., 1927.
40. Cavanaugh, Rev. William Thomas, C.P., J.U.D., The Reservation of the Blessed Sacrament, VIII-101 pp., 1927.

41. Doheny, Rev. William J., C.S.C., A.B., J.C.D., Church Property: Modes of Acquisition, X-118 pp., 1927.
42. Feldhaus, Rev. Aloysius H., C.PP.S., J.C.D., Oratories, IX-141 pp., 1927.
43. Kelly, Rev. James Patrick, A.B., J.C.D., The Jurisdiction of the Simple Confessor, X-208 pp., 1927.
44. Neuberger, Rev. Nicholas J., J.C.D., Canon 6 or the Relation of the Codex Juris Canonici to the Preceding Legislation, V-95 pp., 1927.
45. O'Keefe, Rev. Gerald Michael, J.C.D., Matrimonial Dispensations, Powers of Bishops, Priests, and Confessors, VIII-232 pp., 1927.
46. Quigley, Rev. Joseph A. M., A.B., J.C.D., Condemned Societies, 139 pp., 1927.
47. Zaplotnik, Rev. Johannes Leo, J.C.D., De Vicariis Foraneis, X-142 pp., 1927.
48. Duskie, Rev. John Aloysius, A.B., J.C.D., The Canonical Status of the Orientals in the United States, VIII-196 pp., 1928.
49. Hyland, Rev. Francis Edward, J.C.D., Excommunication, Its Nature, Historical Development and Effects, VIII-181 pp., 1928.
50. Reinmann, Rev. Gerald Joseph, O.M.C., J.C.D., The Third Order Secular of Saint Francis, 201 pp., 1928.
51. Schenk, Rev. Francis J., J.C.D., The Matrimonial Impediments of Mixed Religion and Disparity of Cult, XVI-318 pp., 1929.
52. Coady, Rev. John Joseph, S.T.D., J.U.D., A.M., The Appointment of Pastors, VIII-150 pp., 1929.
53. Kay, Rev. Thomas Henry, J.C.D., Competence in Matrimonial Procedure, VIII-164 pp., 1929.
54. Turner, Rev. Sidney Joseph, C.P., J.U.D., The Vow of Poverty, XLIX-217 pp., 1929.
55. Kearney, Rev. Raymond A., A.B., S.T.D., J.C.D., The Principles of Delegation, VII-149 pp., 1929.
56. Conran, Rev. Edward James, A.B., J.C.D., The Interdict, V-163 pp., 1930.
57. O'Neill, Rev. William H., J.C.D., Papal Rescripts of Favor, VII-218 pp., 1930.
58. Bastnagel, Rev. Clement Vincent, J.U.D., The Appointment of Parochial Adjutants and Assistants, XV-257 pp., 1930.
59. Ferry, Rev. William A., A.B., J.C.D., Stole Fees, V-136 pp., 1930.
60. Costello, Rev. John Michael, A.B., J.C.D., Domicile and Quasi-Domicile, VII-201 pp., 1930.
61. Kremer, Rev. Michael Nicholas, A.B., S.T.B., J.C.D., Church Support in the United States, VI-136 pp., 1930.
62. Angulo, Rev. Luis, C.M., J.C.D., Legislation de la Iglesia sobre la intencion en la application de la Santa Misa, VII-104 pp., 1931.
63. Frey, Rev. Wolfgang Norbert, O.S.B., A.B., J.C.D., The Act of Religious Profession, VIII-174 pp., 1931.

64. Roberts, Rev. James Brendan, A.B., J.C.D., The Banns of Marriage, XIV-140 pp., 1931.
65. Ryder, Rev. Raymond Aloysius, A.B., J.C.D., Simony, IX-151 pp., 1931.
66. Campagna, Rev. Angelo, Ph.D., J.U.D., Il Vicario Generale del Vescovo, VII-205 pp., 1931.
67. Cox, Rev. Joseph Godfrey, A.B., J.C.D., The Administration of Seminaries, VI-124 pp., 1931.
68. Gregory, Rev. Donald J., J.U.D., The Pauline Privilege, XV-165 pp., 1931.
69. Donohue, Rev. John F., J.C.D., The Impediment of Crime, VII-110 pp., 1931.
70. Dooley, Rev. Eugene A., O.M.I., J.C.D., Church Law on Sacred Relics, IX-143 pp., 1931.
71. Orth, Rev. Clement Raymond, O.M.C., J.C.D., The Approbation of Religious Institutes, 171 pp., 1931.
72. Pernicone, Rev. Joseph M., A.B., J.C.D., The Ecclesiastical Prohibition of Books, XII-267 pp., 1932.
73. Clinton, Rev. Connell, A.B., J.C.D., The Paschal Precept, IX-108 pp., 1932.
74. Donnelly, Rev. Francis B., A.M., S.T.L., J.C.D., The Diocesan Synod, VIII-125 pp., 1932.
75. Torrente, Rev. Camilo, C.M.F., J.C.D., Las Procesiones Sagradas, V-145 pp., 1932.
76. Murphy, Rev. Edwin J., C.PP.S., J.C.D., Suspension Ex Informata Conscientia, XI-122 pp., 1932.
77. MacKenzie, Rev. Eric F., A.M., S.T.L., J.C.D., The Delict of Heresy in its Commission, Penalization, Absolution, VII-124 pp., 1932.
78. Lyons, Rev. Avitus E., S.T.B., J.C.D., The Collegiate Tribunal of First Instance, XI-147 pp., 1932.
79. Connolly, Rev. Thomas A., J.C.D., Appeals, XI-195, pp., 1932.
80. Sangmeister, Rev. Joseph V., A.B., J.C.D., Force and Fear as Precluding Matrimonial Consent, V-211 pp., 1932.
81. Jaeger, Rev. Leo A., A.B., J.C.D., The Administration of Vacant and Quasi-Vacant Episcopal Sees in the United States, IX-229 pp., 1932.
82. Rimlinger, Rev. Herbert T., J.C.D., Error Invalidating Matrimonial Consent, VII-79 pp., 1932.
83. Barrett, Rev. John D. M., S.S., J.C.D., A Comparative Study of the Councils of Baltimore and the Code of Canon Law, IX-223 pp., 1932.
84. Carberry, Rev. John J., Ph.D., S.T.D., J.C.D., The Juridical Form of Marriage, X-177 pp., 1934.
85. Dolan, Rev. John L., A.B., J.C.D., The Defensor Vinculi, XII-157 pp., 1934.
86. Hannan, Rev. Jerome D., A.M., S.T.D., LL.B., J.C.D., The Canon Law of Wills, IX-517 pp., 1934.

87. LEMIEUX, REV. DELISE A., A.M., J.C.D., The Sentence in Ecclesiastical Procedure, IX-131 pp., 1934.
88. O'ROURKE, REV. JAMES J., A.B., J.C.D., Parish Registers, VII-109 pp., 1934.
89. TIMLIN, REV. BARTHOLOMEW, O.F.M., A.M., J.C.D., Conditional Matrimonial Consent, X-381 pp., 1934.
90. WAHL, REV. FRANCIS X., A.B., J.C.D., The Matrimonial Impediments of Consanguinity and Affinity, VI-125 pp., 1934.
91. WHITE, REV. ROBERT J., A.B., LL.B., S.T.B., J.C.D., Canonical Ante-Nuptial Promises and the Civil Law, VI-152 pp., 1934.
92. HERRERA, REV. ANTONIO PARRA, O.C.D., J.C.D., Legislacion Ecclesiastica sobra el Ayūno y la Abstinencia, XI-191 pp., 1935.
93. KENNEDY, REV. EDWIN J., J.C.D., The Special Matrimonial Process in Cases of Evident Nullity, X-165 pp., 1935.
94. MANNING, REV. JOHN J., A.B., J.C.D., Presumption of Law in Matrimonial Procedure, XI-111 pp., 1935.
95. MOEDER, REV. JOHN M., J.C.D., The Proper Bishop for Ordination and Dismissorial Letters, VII-135 pp., 1935.
96. O'MARA, REV. WILLIAM A., A.B., J.C.D., Canonical Causes for Matrimonial Dispensations, IX-155 pp., 1935.
97. REILLY, REV. PETER, J.C.D., Residence of Pastors, IX-81 pp., 1935.
98. SMITH, REV. MARINER T., O.P., S.T.Lr., J.C.D., The Penal Law for Religious, VIII-169 pp., 1935.
99. WHALEN, REV. DONALD W., A.M., J.C.D., The Value of Testimonial Evidence in Matrimonial Procedure, XIII-297 pp., 1935.
100. CLEARY, REV. JOSEPH F., J.C.D., Canonical Limitations on the Alienation of Church Property, VIII-141 pp., 1936.
101. GLYNN, REV. JOHN C., J.C.D., The Promoter of Justice, XX-337 pp., 1936.
102. BRENNAN, REV. JAMES H., S.S., M.A., S.T.B., J.C.D., The Simple Convalidation of Marriage, VI-135 pp., 1937.
103. BRUNINI, REV. JOSEPH BERNARD, J.C.D., The Clerical Obligations of Canons 139 and 142, X-121 pp., 1937.
104. CONNOR, REV. MAURICE, A.B., J.C.D., The Administrative Removal of Pastors, VIII-159 pp., 1937.
105. GUILFOYLE, REV. MERLIN JOSEPH, J.C.D., Custom, XI-144 pp., 1937.
106. HUGHES, REV. JAMES AUSTIN, A.B., A.M., J.C.D., Witnesses in Criminal Trials of Clerics, IX-140 pp., 1937.
107. JANSEN, REV. RAYMOND J., A.B., S.T.L., J.C.D., Canonical Provisions for Catechetical Instruction, VII-153 pp., 1937.
108. KEALY, REV. JOHN JAMES, A.B., J.C.D., The Introductory Libellus in Church Court Procedure, XI-121 pp., 1937.
109. MCMANUS, REV. JAMES EDWARD, C.SS.R., J.C.D., The Administration of Temporal Goods in Religious Institutes, XVI-196 pp., 1937.

110. Moriarty, Rev. Eugene James, J.C.D., Oaths in Ecclesiastical Courts, X-115 pp., 1937.
111. Rainer, Rev. Elicius George, C.SS.R., J.C.D., Suspension of Clerics, XVII-249 pp., 1937.
112. Reilly, Rev. Thomas F., C.SS.R., J.C.D., Visitation of Religious, VI-195 pp., 1938.
113. Moriarty, Rev. Francis E., C.SS.R., J.C.D., The Extraordinary Absolution from Censures, XV-334 pp., 1938.
114. Connolly, Rev. Nicholas P., J.C.D., The Canonical Erection of Parishes, X-132 pp., 1938.
115. Donovan, Rev. James Joseph, J.C.D., The Pastor's Obligation in Prenuptial Investigation, XII-322 pp., 1938.
116. Harrigan, Rev. Robert J., M.A., S.T.B., J.C.D., The Radical Sanation of Invalid Marriages, VIII-208 pp., 1938.
117. Boffa, Rev. Conrad Humbert, J.C.D., Canonical Provisions for Catholic Schools, VII-211 pp., 1939.
118. Parsons, Rev. Anscar John, O.M.Cap., J.C.D., Canonical Elections, XII-236 pp., 1939.
119. Reilly, Rev. Edward Michael, A.B., J.C.D., The General Norms of Dispensation, XII-156 pp., 1939.
120. Ryan, Rev. Gerald Aloysius, A.B., J.C.D., Principles of Episcopal Jurisdiction, XII-172 pp., 1939.
121. Burton, Rev. Francis James, C.S.C., A.B., J.C.D., A Commentary on Canon 1125, X-222 pp., 1940.
122. Miaskiewicz, Rev. Francis Sigismund, J.C.D., Supplied Jurisdiction According to Canon 209, XII-340 pp., 1940.
123. Rice, Rev. Patrick William, A.B., J.C.D., Proof of Death in Prenuptial Investigation, VIII-156 pp., 1940.
124. Anglin, Rev. Thomas Francis, M.S., J.C.D., The Eucharistic Fast, VIII-183 pp., 1941.
125. Coleman, Rev. John Jerome, J.C.D., The Minister of Confirmation, VI-153 pp., 1941.
126. Downs, Rev. John Emmanuel, A.B., J.C.D., The Concept of Clerical Immunity, XI-163 pp., 1941.
127. Esswein, Rev. Anthony Albert, J.C.D., Extrajudicial Penal Powers of Ecclesiastical Superiors, X-144 pp., 1941.
128. Farrell, Rev. Benjamin Francis, M.A., S.T.L., J.C.D., The Rights and Duties of the Local Ordinary Regarding Congregations of Women Religious of Pontifical Approval, V-195 pp., 1941.
129. Feeney, Rev. Thomas John, A.B., S.T.L., J.C.D., Restitutio in Integrum, VI-169 pp., 1941.
130. Findlay, Rev. Stephen William, O.S.B., A.B., J.C.D., Canonical Norms Governing the Deposition and Degradation of Clerics, XVII-279 pp., 1941.

131. GOODWINE, REV. JOHN, A.B., S.T.L., J.C.D., The Right of the Church to Acquire Property, VIII-119 pp., 1941.
132. HESTON, REV. EDWARD LOUIS, C.S.C., Ph.D., S.T.D., J.C.D., The Alienation of Church Property in the United States, XII-222 pp., 1941.
133. HOGAN, REV. JAMES JOHN, A.B., S.T.L., J.C.D., Judicial Advocates and Procurators, XIII-200 pp., 1941.
134. KEALY, REV. THOMAS M., A.B., Litt.B., J.C.D., Dowry of Women Religious, IX-152 pp., 1941.
135. KEENE, REV. MICHAEL JAMES, O.S.B., J.C.D., Religious Ordinaries and Canon 198, V-164 pp., 1941 (printed 1942).
136. KERIN, REV. CHARLES A., S.S., M.A., S.T.B., J.C.D., The Privation of Christian Burial, XVI-279 pp., 1941.
137. LOUIS, REV. WILLIAM FRANCIS, M.A., J.C.D., Diocesan Archives, X-101 pp., 1941.
138. McDEVITT, REV. GILBERT JOSEPH, A.B., J.C.D., Legitimacy and Legitimation, X-247 pp., 1941.
139. McDONOUGH, REV. THOMAS JOSEPH, A.B., J.C.D., Apostolic Administrators, X-217 pp., 1941.
140. MEIER, REV. CARL ANTHONY, A.B., J.C.D., Penal Administrative Procedure Against Negligent Pastors, XI-240 pp., 1941.
141. SCHMIDT, REV. JOHN ROGG, A.B., J.C.D., The Principles of Authentic Interpretation in Canon 17 of the Code of Canon Law, XII-331 pp., 1941.
142. SLAFKOSKY, REV. ANDREW LEONARD, A.B., J.C.D., The Canonical Episcopal Visitation of the Diocese, X-197 pp., 1941.
143. SWOBODA, REV. INNOCENT ROBERT, O.F.M., J.C.D., Ignorance in Relation to the Imputability of Delicts, IX-271 pp., 1941.
144. DUBÉ, REV. ARTHUR JOSEPH, A.B., J.C.D., The General Principles for the Reckoning of Time in Canon Law, VIII-299 pp., 1941.
145. McBRIDE, REV. JAMES T., A.B., J.C.D., Incardination and Excardination of Seculars, XX-585 pp., 1941.
146. KRÓL, REV. JOHN T., J.C.D., The Defendant in Ecclesiastical Trials, XII-207 pp., 1942.
147. COMYNS, REV. JOSEPH J., C.SS.R., A.B., J.C.D., Papal and Episcopal Administration of Church Property, XIV-155 pp., 1942.
148. BARRY, REV. GARRETT FRANCIS, O.M.I., J.C.D., Violation of the Cloister, XII-260 pp., 1942.
149. BOLDUC, REV. GATIEN, C.S.V., A.B., S.T.L., J.C.D., Les Études dans les Religions Cléricales, VIII-155 pp., 1942.
150. BOYLE, REV. DAVID JOHN, M.A., J.C.D., The Juridic Effects of Moral Certitude on Pre-Nuptial Guarantees, XII-188 pp., 1942.
151. CANAVAN, REV. WALTER JOSEPH, M.A., Litt.D., J.C.D., The Profession of Faith, XII-143 pp., 1942.
152. DESROCHERS, REV. BRUNO, A.B., Ph.L., S.T.B., J.C.D., Le Premier Concile Plénier de Québec et le Code de Droit Canonique, XIV-186 pp., 1942.

153. DILLON, REV. ROBERT EDWARD, A.B., J.C.D., Common Law Marriage, X-148 pp., 1942.

154. DODWELL, REV. EDWARD JOHN, Ph.D., S.T.B., J.C.D., The Time and Place for the Celebration of Marriage, X-156 pp., 1942.

155. DONNELLAN, REV. THOMAS ANDREW, A.B., J.C.D., The Obligation of the Missa pro Populo, VII-131 pp., 1942.

156. ELTZ, REV. LOUIS ANTHONY, A.B., J.C.D., Cooperation in Crime, XII-208 pp., 1942.

157. GASS, REV. SYLVESTER FRANCIS, M.A., J.C.D., Ecclesiastical Pensions, XI-206 pp., 1942.

158. GUINIVEN, REV. JOHN JOSEPH, C.SS.R., J.C.D., The Precept of Hearing Mass, XIV-188 pp., 1942.

159. GULCZYNSKI, REV. JOHN THEOPHILUS, J.C.D., The Desecration and Violation of Churches, X-126 pp., 1942.

160. HAMMILL, REV. JOHN LEO, M.A., J.C.D., The Obligations of the Traveler According to Canon 14, VIII-204 pp., 1942.

161. HAYDT, REV. JOHN JOSEPH, A.B., J.C.D., Reserved Benefices, XI-148 pp., 1942.

162. HUSER, REV. ROGER JOHN, O.F.M., A.B., J.C.D., The Crime of Abortion in Canon Law, XII-187 pp., 1942.

163. KEARNEY, REV. FRANCIS PATRICK, A.B., S.T.L., J.C.D., The Principles of Canon 1127, X-162 pp., 1942.

164. LINAHEN, REV. LEO JAMES, S.T.L., J.C.D., De Absolutione Complicis in Peccato Turpi, V-114 pp., 1942.

165. MCCLOSKEY, REV. JOSEPH ALOYSIUS, A.B., J.C.D., The Subject of Ecclesiastical Law According to Canon 12, XVII-246 pp., 1942 (printed 1943).

166. O'NEILL, REV. FRANCIS JOSEPH, C.SS.R., J.C.D., The Dismissal of Religious in Temporary Vows, XIII-220 pp., 1942.

167. PRINCE, REV. JOHN EDWARD, A.B., S.T.B., J.C.D., The Diocesan Chancellor, X-136 pp., 1942.

168. RIESNER, REV. ALBERT JOSEPH, C.SS.R., J.C.D., Apostates and Fugitives from Religious Institutes, IX-168 pp., 1942.

169. STENGER, REV. JOSEPH BERNARD, J.C.D., The Mortgaging of Church Property, 186 pp., 1942.

170. WALDRON, REV. JOSEPH FRANCIS, A.B., J.C.D., The Minister of Baptism, XII-197 pp., 1942.

171. WILLETT, REV. ROBERT ALBERT, J.C.D., The Probative Value of Documents in Ecclesiastical Trials, X-124 pp., 1942.

172. WOEBER, REV. EDWARD MARTIN, M.A., J.C.D., The Interpellations, XII-161 pp., 1942.

173. BENKO, REV. MATTHEW ALOYSIUS, O.S.B., M.A., J.C.D., The Abbot *Nullius*, XVI-148 pp., 1943.

174. CHRIST, REV. JOSEPH JAMES, M.A., S.T.L., J.C.D., Dispensation from Vindicative Penalties, XIV-285 pp., 1943.
175. CLANCY, REV. PATRICK M. J., O.P., A.B., S.T.Lr., J.C.D., The Local Religious Superior, X-229 pp., 1943.
176. CLARKE, REV. THOMAS JAMES, J.C.D., Parish Societies, XII-147 pp., 1943.
177. CONNOLLY, REV. JOHN PATRICK, S.T.L., J.C.D., Synodal Examiners and Parish Priest Consultors, X-223 pp., 1943.
178. DRUMM, REV. WILLIAM MARTIN, A.B., J.C.D., Hospital Chaplains, XII-175 pp., 1943.
179. FLANAGAN, REV. BERNARD JOSEPH, A.B., S.T.L., J.C.D., The Canonical Erection of Religious Houses, X-147 pp., 1943.
180. KELLEHER, REV. STEPHEN JOSEPH, A.B., S.T.B., J.C.D., Discussions with Non-Catholics: Canonical Legislation, X-93 pp., 1943.
181. LEWIS, REV. GORDIAN, C.P., J.C.D., Chapters in Religious Institutes, XII-169 pp., 1943.
182. MARX, REV. ADOLPH, J.C.D., The Declaration of Nullity of Marriages Contracted Outside the Church, X-151 pp., 1943.
183. MATULENAS, REV. RAYMOND ANTHONY, O.S.B., A.B., J.C.D., Communication, a Source of Privileges, XII-225 pp., 1943.
184. O'LEARY, REV. CHARLES GERARD, C.SS.R., J.C.D., Religious Dismissed After Perpetual Profession, X-213 pp., 1943.
185. POWER, REV. CORNELIUS MICHAEL, J.C.D., The Blessing of Cemeteries, XII-231 pp., 1943.
186. SHUHLER, REV. RALPH VINCENT, O.S.A., J.C.D., Privileges of Religious to Absolve and Dispense, XII-195 pp., 1943.
187. ZIOLKOWSKI, REV. THADDEUS STANISLAUS, A.B., J.C.D., The Consecration and Blessing of Churches, XII-151 pp., 1943.
188. HENEGHAN, REV. JOHN JOSEPH, S.T.D., J.C.D., The Marriages of Unworthy Catholics: Canons 1065 and 1066, XVI-213 pp., 1944.
189. CARROLL, REV. COLEMAN FRANCIS, M.A., S.T.L., J.C.L., Charitable Institutions.
190. CIESLUK, REV. JOSEPH EDWARD, PH.B., S.T.L., J.C.D., National Parishes in the United States, VI-178 pp., 1944.
191. COBURN, REV. VINCENT PAUL, A.B., J.C.D., Marriages of Conscience, XII-172 pp., 1944.
192. CONNORS, REV. CHARLES PAUL, C.S.SP., A.B., J.C.D., Extra-Judicial Procurators in the Code of Canon Law, X-94 pp., 1944.
193. COYLE, REV. PAUL RAYMOND, A.B., J.C.D., Judicial Exceptions, X-142 pp., 1944.
194. FAIR, REV. BARTHOLOMEW FRANCIS, A.B., S.T.L., J.C.D., The Impediment of Abduction, XII-122 pp., 1944.
195. GALLAGHER, REV. THOMAS RAPHAEL, O.P., A.B., S.T.LR., J.C.D., The Examination of the Qualities of the Ordinand, X-166 pp., 1944.

196. Gannon, Rev. John Mark, S.T.L., J.C.D., The Interstices Required for the Promotion to Orders, XII-100 pp., 1944.
197. Goldsmith, Rev. J. William, B.C.S., S.T.L., J.C.D., The Competence of Church and State Over Marriages—Disputed Points, X-128 pp., 1944.
198. Goodwine, Rev. Joseph Gerard, A.B., S.T.B., J.C.D., The Reception of Converts, XIV-326 pp., 1944.
199. Kowalski, Rev. Romuald Eugene, O.F.M., A.B., J.C.D., Sustenance of Religious Houses of Regulars, X-174 pp., 1944.
200. McCoy, Rev. Alan Edward, O.F.M., J.C.D., Force and Fear in Relation to Delictual Imputability and Penal Responsibility, XII-160 pp., 1944.
201. McDevitt, Rev. Vincent John, Ph.B., S.T.L., J.C.L., Perjury.
202. Martin, Rev. Thomas Owen, Ph.D., S.T.D., J.C.D., Adverse Possession, Prescription and Limitation of Actions: The Canonical "Praescriptio," XX-208 pp., 1944.
203. Miklosovic, Rev. Paul John, A.B., J.C.L., Attempted Marriages and Their Consequent Juridic Effects.
204. Mundy, Rev. Thomas Maurice, A.B., S.T.L., J.C.D., The Union of Parishes, X-164 pp., 1944.
205. O'Dea, Rev. John Coyle, A.B., J.C.D., The Matrimonial Impediment of Nonage, VIII-126 pp., 1944.
206. Olalia, Rev. Alexander Ayson, S.T.L., J.C.D., A Comparative Study of the Christian Constitution of States and the Constitution of the Philippine Commonwealth, XII-136 pp., 1944.
207. Poisson, Rev. Pierre-Marie, C.S.C., A.B., Ph.L., Th.L., J.C.L., Droits Patrimoniaux des Maisons et des Eglises Religieuses.
208. Stadalnikas, Rev. Casimir Joseph, M.I.C., J.C.D., Reservation of Censures, X-141 pp., 1944.
209. Sullivan, Rev. Eugene Henry, S.T.L., J.C.D., Proof of the Reception of the Sacraments, X-165 pp., 1944.
210. Vaughan, Rev. William Edward, J.C.D., Constitutions for Diocesan Courts, X-210 pp., 1944.
211. Paro, Rev. Gino, S.T.D., J.C.D., The Right of Papal Legation, X-221 pp., 1944 (printed 1947).
212. Balzer, Rev. Ralph Francis, C.P., J.C.D., The Computation of Time in a Canonical Novitiate, X-227 pp., 1945.
213. Dougherty, Rev. John Whelan, A.B., S.T.L., J.C.D., De Inquisitione Speciali, XII-195 pp., 1945.
214. Dziob, Rev. Michael Walter, J.C.D., The Sacred Congregation for the Oriental Church, XII-181 pp., 1945.
215. Eidenschink, Rev. John Albert, O.S.B., B.A., J.C.D., The Election of Bishops in the Letters of Pope Gregory the Great, VIII-200 pp., 1945.
216. Gill, Rev. Nicholas, C.P., J.C.D., The Spiritual Prefect in Clerical Religious Houses of Study, X-140 pp., 1945.

217. HYNES, REV. HARRY GERARD, S.T.L., J.C.D., The Privileges of Cardinals, XII-183 pp., 1945.
218. MCDEVITT, REV. GERALD VINCENT, S.T.L., J.C.D., The Renunciation of an Ecclesiastical Office, XIV-179 pp., 1945.
219. MANNING, REV. JOSEPH LEROY, J.C.D., The Free Conferral of Offices, VII-116 pp., 1945.
220. MEYER, REV. LOUIS G., O.S.B., A.B., S.T.B., J.C.D., Alms-gathering by Religious, XII-163 pp., 1945.
221. O'DONNELL, REV. CLETUS FRANCIS, M.A., J.C.D., The Marriage of Minors, XII-268 pp., 1945.
222. PRUNSKIS, REV. JOSEPH, J.C.D., Comparative Law, Ecclesiastical and Civil, in Lithuanian Concordat, X-161 pp., 1945.
223. SWEENEY, REV. FRANCIS PATRICK, C.SS.R., J.C.D., The Reduction of Clerics to the Lay State, X-199 pp., 1945.
224. VOGELPOHL, REV. HENRY JOHN, J.C.D., The Simple Impediments to Holy Orders, XVI-190 pp., 1945.
225. BROCKHAUS, REV. THOMAS AQUINAS, O.S.B., J.C.D., Religious who are known as *Conversi*, X-127 pp., 1945.
226. GRIESE, REV. ORVILLE NICHOLAS, S.T.D., J.C.D., The Marriage Contract and the Procreation of Offspring, XVI-224 pp., 1946.
227. BOUDREAUX, REV. WARREN LOUIS, J.C.D., The *"ab acatholicis nati"* of Canon 1099, § 2, XII-110 pp., 1946.
228. BOWE, REV. THOMAS JOSEPH, A.B., J.C.D., Religious Superioresses, VIII-206 pp., 1946.
229. DIEDERICHS, REV. MICHAEL FERDINAND, S.C.J., J.C.D., The Jurisdiction of the Latin Ordinaries over their Oriental Subjects, XIV-153 pp., 1946.
230. DINGMAN, REV. MAURICE JOHN, A.B., S.T.L., J.C.L., The Plaintiff in Contentious Trials.
231. FRISON, REV. BASIL, C.M.F., M.MUS., J.C.D., The Retroactivity of Law, X-221 pp., 1946.
232. GALVIN, REV. WILLIAM ANTHONY, M.A., J.C.D., The Administrative Transfer of Pastors, XII-288 pp., 1946.
233. GORACY, REV. JOSEPH C., J.C.L., The Diriment Matrimonial Impediment of Major Orders.
234. HALE, REV. JOSEPH FRANCIS, M.A., S.T.L., J.C.D., The Pastor of Burial, X-247 pp., 1946 (printed 1949).
235. HENRY, REV. JOSEPH ARTHUR, A.B., J.C.D., The Mass and Holy Communion: Interritual Law, XII-138 pp., 1946.
236. LINENBERGER, REV. HERBERT, C.PP.S., J.C.D., The False Denunciation of an Innocent Confessor, VIII-205 pp., 1946 (printed 1949).
237. LOWRY, REV. JAMES MARTIN, A.B., J.C.D., Dispensation from Private Vows, XII-266 pp., 1946.
238. LYNCH, REV. GEORGE EDWARD, A.B., S.T.L., J.C.D., Coadjutors and Auxiliaries of Bishops, X-107 pp., 1946 (printed 1947).

239. LYNCH, REV. TIMOTHY, M.S.SS.T., J.C.D., Contracts between Bishops and Religious Congregations, XIII-232 pp., 1946.
240. MCCLUNN, REV. JUSTIN DAVID, A.B., S.T.L., J.C.D., Administrative Recourse, VII-142 pp., 1946.
241. LOHMULLER, REV. MARTIN NICHOLAS, A.B., J.C.D., The Promulgation of Law, XII-140 pp., 1947.
242. MCGRATH, REV. JAMES, A.B., J.C.D., The Privilege of the Canon, XII-156 pp., 1946.
243. MARBACH, REV. JOSEPH FRANCIS, A.B., J.C.D., Marriage Legislation for the Catholics of the Oriental Rites in the United States and Canada, XIV-314 pp., 1946.
244. SHIMKUS, REV. BERNARD ALOYSIUS, A.B., J.C.L., The Determination and Transfer of Rite.
245. SMITH, REV. VINCENT MICHAEL, A.B., S.T.L., J.C.L., Ignorance Affecting Matrimonial Consent.
246. WACHTRLE, REV. PAUL ANTHONY, A.B., J.C.L., The Baptism of the Children of Non-Catholics.
247. CROTTY, REV. MATTHEW MICHAEL, J.C.D., The Recipient of First Holy Communion, X-142 pp., 1947.
248. EAGLETON, REV. GEORGE, J.C.D., The Quinquennial Faculties, Formula IV, XIV-199 pp., 1947 (printed 1948).
249. GIBBONS, REV. MARION LEO, C.M., J.C.L., Domicile of the Wife Unlawfully Separated from Her Husband, XIV-171 pp., 1947.
250. KELLY, REV. BERNARD M., S.T.L., J.C.D., The Functions Reserved to Pastors, XII-141 pp., 1947.
251. KILCULLEN, REV. THOMAS J., LL.M., J.C.D., The Collegiate Moral Person as Party Litigant, X-150 pp., 1947.
252. LAFONTAINE, REV. GERMAINE JOSEPH, W.F., J.C.D., Relations Canoniques entre le Missionaire et Ses Superieurs, X-117 pp., 1947.
253. LANE, REV. LORAS THOMAS, A.B., S.T.L., J.C.D., Matrimonial Procedure in the Ordinary Court of Second Instance, XVI-184 pp., 1947.
254. LOVER, REV. JAMES FRANCIS, C.Ss.R., J.C.D., The Master of Novices, X-168 pp., 1947.
255. MCNICHOLAS, REV. TIMOTHY JOSEPH, J.C.L., The *Septimae Manus* Witness.
256. MAROSITZ, REV. JOSEPH JOHN, M.S.C., J.C.D., Obligations and Privileges of Religious Promoted to the Episcopal or Cardinalitial Dignities, XII-180 pp., 1947.
257. MURPHY, REV. FRANCIS JOSEPH, J.C.D., Legislative Powers of the Provincial Council, XII-158 pp., 1947.
258. O'BRIEN, REV. ROMAEUS WILLIAM, O.Carm., J.C.D., The Provincial Superior in Religious Orders of Men, X-294 pp., 1947.
259. PFALLER, REV. BENEDICT ANTHONY, O.S.B., J.C.D., *The ipso facto* Effected Dismissal of Religious, XII-225 pp., 1947.

260. POPEK, REV. ALPHONSE SYLVESTER, J.C.D., The Rights and Obligations of Metropolitans, XX-460 pp., 1947.
261. RISTUCCIA, REV. BERNARD JOSEPH, C.M., J.C.D., Quasi-Religious, XVI-318 pp., 1947 (printed 1949).
262. SONNTAG, REV. NATHANIEL LOUIS, O.F.M.Cap., J.C.D., Censorship of Special Classes of Books, XII-147 pp., 1947.
263. STADLER, REV. JOSEPH NICHOLAS, J.C.D., Frequent Holy Communion, X-158 pp., 1947.
264. SZAL, REV. IGNATIUS JOSEPH, J.C.D., The Communication of Catholics with Schismatics, XII-217 pp., 1947.
265. WAGNER, REV. URBAN S., O.F.M. Conv., J.C.D., Parochial Substitute Vicars and Supplying Priests, IX-126 pp., 1947.
266. QUINN, REV. JOSEPH, M.A., J.C.D., Documents Required for the Reception of Orders, XIV-207 pp., 1948.
267. BENNINGTON, REV. JAMES CLEMENT, A.B., J.C.L., The Recipient of Confirmation.
268. BLAHER, REV. DAMIAN JOSEPH, O.F.M., A.B., J.C.L., The Ordinary Processes in Causes of Beatification and Canonization.
269. CLUNE, REV. ROBERT BELL, B.A., J.C.L., The Judicial Interrogation of the Parties.
270. COURTEMANCHE, REV. BASIL F., B.A., J.C.L., The Total Simulation of Matrimonial Consent.
271. DLOUHY, REV. MAUR JOHN, O.S.B., A.B., J.C.L., The Ordination of Exempt Religious.
272. DONOVAN, REV. JOHN THOMAS, PH.B., S.T.L., J.C.D., The Clerical Obligation of Canons 138 and 140, XII-209 pp., 1948.
273. FREKING, REV. FREDERICK W., A.B., S.T.B., J.C.L., The Canonical Installation of Pastors.
274. FULTON, REV. THOMAS B., J.C.L., Prenuptial Investigation.
275. GODLEY, REV. JAMES P., J.C.L., Time and Place for the Celebration of Mass.
276. KANE, REV. THOMAS A., A.B., B.S., J.C.D., Jurisdiction of the Patriarchs of the Major Sees, XII-153 pp., 1948 (printed 1949).
277. KENNEDY, REV. ANDREW A., J.C.L., The Annual Pastoral Report to the Local Ordinary.
278. KONRAD, REV. JOSEPH GEORGE, J.C.L., Transfer of Religious.
279. KRESS, REV. ALPHONSE, J.C.L., Contumacy in Ecclesiastical Trials.
280. MCCARTNEY, REV. MARCELLUS ANTHONY, O.F.M., M.A., J.C.L., Faculties of Regular Confessors.
281. MCCASLIN, REV. EDWARD PATRICK, M.A., S.T.L., J.C.L., The Division of Parishes.
282. MCELROY, REV. FRANCIS J., A.B., J.C.L., The Privileges of Bishops.

283. Quinn, Rev. Stephen, M.S.SS.T., J.C.D., Relation Between the Local Ordinary and Religious of Diocesan Approval, XII-153 pp., 1948 (printed 1949).
284. Schneider, Rev. Edelhard Louis, S.D.S., B.A., J.C.D., The Status of Secularized Ex-Religious Clerics, X-155 pp., 1948.
285. Thompson, Chester J., A.B., J.C.L., The Simple Removal from Office.
286. O'Brien, Rev. Kenneth R., A.B., J.C.D., The Nature of Support of Diocesan Priests in the United States, XVI-162 pp., 1949.
287. Metz, Rev. John E., S.T.L., J.C.D., The Recording Judge in the Ecclesiastical Collegiate Tribunal, X-130 pp., 1949.
288. Reinhardt, Rev. Marion J., S.T.L., J.C.L., The Rogatory Commission.
289. Ortega Uhiuk, Rev. Juan, S.J., J.C.L., De Delicto Sollicitationis.
290. Casey, Rev. James V., J.C.D., A Study of Canon 2222 § 1, XII-127 pp., 1949.
291. Allgeier, Rev. Joseph L., J.C.L., The Canonical Obligation of Preaching in Parish Churches.
292. Cahill, Rev. Daniel R., J.C.L., The Custody of the Holy Eucharist.
293. Carr, Rev. Aiden, O.F.M. Conv., S.T.D., J.C.L., Vocation to the Priesthood: Its Canonical Concept.
294. Knopke, Rev. Roch F., O.F.M., J.C.L., Reverential Fear in Matrimonial Cases in Asiatic Countries: Rota Cases.
295. Lavelle, Rev. Howard D., J.C.L., The Obligation of Holding Sacred Missions in Parishes.
296. Mickells, Rev. Anthony B., J.C.L., The Constitutive Elements of Parishes.
297. Noone, Rev. John J., J.C.L., Nullity in Judicial Acts.
298. Sheehan, Rev. Daniel E., J.C.L., The Minister of Holy Communion.
299. Statkus, Rev. Francis J., J.C.L., The Minister of the Last Sacraments.
300. Cook, Rev. John P., J.C.L., Ecclesiastical Communities and Their Ability to Induce Legal Customs.
301. Fazzalaro, Rev. Francis J., J.C.L., The Place for the Hearing of Confessions.
302. Hannan, Rev. Philip M., J.C.L., The Canonical Concept of *congrua sustentatio* for the Secular Clergy.
303. Quinn, Rev. Hugh G., S.T.L., J.C.L., The Particular Penal Precept.
304. Gallagher, Rev. John F., J.C.L., The Matrimonial Impediment of Public Propriety.
305. Welsh, Rev. Thomas J., J.C.L., The Use of the Portable Altar.

www.ingramcontent.com/pod-product-compliance
Lightning Source LLC
LaVergne TN
LVHW050220080826
844660LV00012B/440

* 9 7 8 0 8 1 3 2 2 4 7 1 8 *